CRITICAL W9-BRJ-219

12 Sermons
on the Love of Christ

Charles H. Spurgeon

Baker Books

A Division of Baker Book House Co.
Grand Rapids, Michigan 49516

Reprinted 1977 by Baker Books
a division of Baker Book House Company
P.O. Box 6287, Grand Rapids, MI 49516-6287

ISBN: 0-8010-8096-7

Sixth printing, August 1995

Printed in the United States of America

Contents

1. Oh, How He Loves!

"Then said the Jews, Behold how he loved him ! "—John xi. 36.

It was at the grave of Lazarus that Jesus wept, and his grief was so manifest to the onlookers that they said, "Behold how he loved him!" Most of us here, I trust, are not mere onlookers, but we have a share in the special love of Jesus. We see evidences of that love, not in his tears, but in the precious blood that he so freely shed for us; so we ought to marvel even more than those Jews did at the love of Jesus, and to see further into his heart than they did, and to know more of him than they could in the brief interval in which they had become acquainted with him. When we think of his love to us, we may well cry, "Behold how he has loved us!"

These Jews expressed their wonder at the love that Jesus had for his friend Lazarus; they did not keep that wonder to themselves, but they said, "Behold how he loved him!" In these days, we are too apt to repress our emotions. I cannot say that I greatly admire the way in which some enthusiastic folk shout "Glory!" "Hallelujah!" "Amen," and so on, in the midst of sermons and prayers; yet I would sooner have a measure of that enthusiastic noise than have you constantly stifling your natural emotions, and checking yourself from giving utterance to your heart's true feelings. If we were in a right state of mind and heart, we should often say to one another, "How wondrous has the love of Jesus been to us!" Our conversation with one another, as brethren and sisters in Christ, would often be upon this blessed subject. We waste far too much of our time upon trifles; it would be well if the love of Jesus so engrossed our thoughts that it engrossed our conversation too. I fear that many, who profess to be Christians, go for a whole year, or even longer, without telling out to others what they are supposed to have experienced of the love of Jesus; yet this ought not to be the case. If we were as we should be, one would frequently say to another, "How great is Christ's love to me, my brother! Dost thou also say that it is great to thee?" Such talk as that between the saints on earth would help us to anticipate the time when we shall want no other theme for conversation in the land beyond the river.

I am going just to remind you of some very simple truths in order to excite the hearts of those of you who are coming to the communion to increased love to the dear Lord and Saviour who has loved you so intensely as to die for you. And first, beloved, let us think of *what the love of Christ has done for us;* secondly, of *what his love has done to us;* and then, thirdly, I want to say that I am afraid *our love to Christ will never cause any wonder except on account of the littleness of it.*

I. So, first, let us quietly think over WHAT THE LOVE OF CHRIST HAS DONE FOR US.

When did Christ's love begin to work for us? It was long before we were born, long before the world was created; far, far back, *in eternity, our Saviour gave the first proof of his love to us by espousing our cause.* By his divine foresight, he looked upon human nature as a palace that had been plundered, and broken down, and in its ruins he perceived the owl, the bittern, the dragon, and all manner of unclean things. Who was there to undertake the great work of restoring that ruined palace? No one but the Word, who was with God, and who was God. "He saw that there was no man, and wondered that there was no intercessor: therefore his own arm brought salvation unto him; and his righteousness, it sustained him." Ere the angels began to sing, or the sun, and moon, and stars threw their first beams athwart primeval darkness, Christ espoused the cause of his people, and resolved not only to restore to them all the blessings that he foresaw that they would lose, but also to add to them richer favours than could ever have been theirs except through him. Even from eternity his delights were with the sons of men; and when I think of him, in that far-distant past of which we can form so slight a conception, becoming "the head over all things to the church" which then existed only in the mind of God, my very soul cries out in a rapture of delight, "Behold how he loved us!"

Remember, too, that *in that eternal secret council, the Lord Jesus Christ became the Representative and Surety of his chosen people.* There was to be, in what was then the far remote future, a covenant between God and man; but who was there who was both able and willing to sign that covenant on man's behalf, and to give a guarantee that man's part of that covenant should be fulfilled? Then it was that the Son of God, well knowing all that such a suretyship would involve, undertook to be the Surety for his people, to fulfil the covenant on their behalf, and to meet all its demands which he foresaw that they would be unable to meet. Then the eternal Father gave into Christ's charge the souls that he had chosen unto eternal life though ages, of which we can have so faint an idea, were to elapse before those souls were to be created; and the eternal Son covenanted to redeem all those souls after they had fallen through sin, to keep them by his grace, and to present them "faultless" before the presence of his Father with exceeding joy. Thus, as Jacob became accountable to Laban for the whole flock committed to his charge, Jesus Christ, "that great Shepherd of the sheep, through the blood of the everlasting covenant," undertook to redeem and guard the whole flock entrusted to his care, so that when, at the last great muster, they should pass under the hand of him that telleth them, not one of them should be missing, and the blessed Shepherd-Son should be able to say to his Father, "Those that thou gavest me I have kept, and not one of them is lost." It was in the everlasting covenant that our Lord Jesus Christ became our Representative and Surety, and engaged on our behalf to fulfil all his Father's will; and as we think of this great mystery of mercy, surely all of us who are truly his must exclaim with grateful adoration, "Behold how he loved us!"

I have been speaking of very ancient things, but let us now come to matters that we can more clearly comprehend. In the fulness of time, *our Lord Jesus Christ left the glories of heaven, and took upon him our nature.* We know so little of what the word "heaven" means that we cannot adequately appreciate the tremendous sacrifice that the Son of God must have made in order to become the Son of Mary. The holy angels could understand far better than we can what their Lord and ours gave up when he renounced the royalties of heaven, and all the honour and glory which rightly belonged to him as the Son of the Highest, and left his throne and crown above to be born as the Babe of an earthly mother, yet even to them there were mysteries about his incarnation which they could not fathom; and as they followed the footprints of the Son of man on his wondrous way from the manger to the cross and to the tomb, they must often have been in that most suggestive attitude of which Peter wrote, "which things the angels desire to look into." To us, the incarnation of Christ is one of the greatest marvels in the history of the universe, and we say, with Paul, "Without controversy great is the mystery of godliness: God was manifest in the flesh." The omnipotent Creator took the nature of a creature into indissoluble union with his divine nature; and, marvel of marvels, that creature was man. "He took not on him the nature of angels; but he took on him the seed of Abraham." For an angel to become an emmet, if that were possible, would be nothing at all in comparison with the condescension of Christ in becoming the Babe of Bethlehem; for, after all, angels and emmets are only creatures formed by Christ, working as one of the persons of the ever-blessed Trinity, for John, writing under the inspiration of the Holy Spirit, expressly says, "All things were made by him; and without him was not anything made that was made." O glorious Bridegroom of our hearts, there never was any other love like thine! That the eternal Son of God should leave his Father's side, and stoop so low as to become one with his chosen people, so that Paul could truly write, "We are members of his body, of his flesh, and of his bones," is such a wonder of condescending grace and mercy that we can only exclaim again and again, "Behold how he loved us!"

Then, "being found in fashion as a man," *he took upon himself human sickness and suffering.* All our infirmities that were not sinful Jesus Christ endured,—the weary feet, the aching head, and the palpitating heart, "that it might be fulfilled which was spoken by Esaias the prophet, saying, Himself took our infirmities, and bare our sicknesses." This was a wondrous proof of love, that the ever-blessed Son of God, who needed not to suffer, should have been willing to be compassed with infirmity just like any other man is. "We have not a high priest who cannot be touched with the feeling of our infirmities; but was in all points tempted like as we are, yet without sin."

But if you want to see the love of Jesus at the highest point it ever reached, you must, by faith, gaze upon him when *he took upon himself the sins of all his people,* as Peter writes, "who his own self bare our sins in his own body on the tree." Oh, how could one who was so pure, so absolutely perfect, ever bear so foul a load? Yet he did bear it, and the transfer of his people's sin from them to him was so complete that the inspired prophet wrote, "The Lord hath laid on him the iniquity of us all," and the inspired apostle wrote, "He hath made him to be sin for us, who knew no sin; that we might be made the righteousness of God in him." When a man marries a woman who is deeply in debt, well knowing the burden that he is taking upon himself even though it is enough to crush him all his life, we may well say, "Behold how he loves her!" That was what Christ did for his Church when he took her into an eternal marriage union with himself, although she had incurred such liabilities as could not have been discharged if she had spent all eternity in hell; he took all her debts upon himself, and then paid them unto the uttermost farthing; for we must never forget that, when Christ bore his people's sins, he also bore the full punishment of them. In fulfilment of the great eternal covenant, and in prospect of all the glory and blessing that would follow from Christ's atoning sacrifice, "it pleased the Lord to bruise him; he hath put him to grief." We cannot have the slightest conception of what that bruising and that grief must have been. We do not know what our Lord's physical and mental agonies must have been, yet they were only the shell of his sufferings; his soul-agony was the kernel, and it was that which made him cry, "My God, my God, why hast thou forsaken me?" Then it was that the precious "corn of wheat" fell into the ground and died; and dying, brought forth "much fruit" of which heaven and eternity alone can tell the full tale. I cannot speak of this wondrous mystery as I fain would do, but you who know even in part what it means must join me in saying, "Behold how he loved us!"

Further than that, *Christ has so completely given himself to us that all that he has is ours.* He is the glorious Husband, and his Church is his bride, the Lamb's wife; and there is nothing that he has which is not also hers even now, and which he will not share with her for ever. By a marriage bond which cannot be broken, for he hateth putting away, he hath espoused her unto himself in righteousness and truth, and she shall be one with him throughout eternity. He has gone up to his Father's house to take possession of the many mansions there, not for himself, but for his people; and his constant prayer is, "Father, I will that they also, whom thou hast given me, be with me where I am; that they may behold my glory, which thou hast given me: for thou lovedst me before the foundation of the world." Jesus has an ever-flowing fountain of joy in his heart, but he desires that his joy may be in you if you belong to him, and that your joy may be full; and everything else that he has is yours as much as it is his, so surely you will again join with me in saying, "Behold how he loved us!"

II. Now, secondly, let us consider WHAT CHRIST HAS DONE TO US, for each of his acts of love should cause us to exclaim, "Behold how he loved us!"

Think, dear brethren and sisters in Christ, *how the Lord dealt with us in the days of our unregeneracy.* He called us again and again, but we would not go to him; and the more lovingly he called us, the more resolutely we hardened our hearts, and refused to accept his gracious invitation. With some of us, this refusal lasted for years; and we wonder now that the Lord waited for us so long. If a rich man invites a pauper to a feast, and the poor man is indifferent to the invitation, or positively refuses to accept it, he gets no second invitation, for man does not press his charity upon the needy; but when we even scoffed at our Lord's call, and made all manner of excuses for not coming to the gospel banquet, he would not take our "No" for an answer, but called, and called, again and again, until at last we could hold out no longer, and had to yield to the sweet compulsion of his grace. Do you not remember, beloved, how you received pardon, and justification, and adoption, and the indwelling of the Spirit, and how the many "exceeding great and precious promises" were brought to you, like the various courses at a royal festival served upon golden dishes adorned with priceless gems? Oh, that blessed, blessed day in which you first came and sat among the guests at the great King's table! As you look back upon it, your heart glows in grateful remembrance of Christ's mercy to you, and you cannot help saying, "Behold how he loved us!"

Many days have passed since then, and I ask you now to recollect *what Christ has done to us since we first trusted in him.* Has his love for you cooled in the slightest degree? We have all of us tried that love by our wandering and waywardness, but we have not quenched it, and its fire still burns just as vehemently as at the first. We have, sometimes, fallen so low that our hearts have been like adamant, incapable of emotion; yet Jesus has loved us all the while, and softened our hard hearts as the glorious sun melts the icebergs of the sea. We were like the insensible grass which calls not for the dew, yet the dew of his love gently fell upon us; and though we had not sought it, our heart was refreshed by it. Our Lord has indeed proved how he loved us by the gracious way in which he has borne with our many provocations; and think too, beloved, with what gifts he has enriched us, with what comforts he has sustained us, with what divine energy he has renewed our failing strength, and with what blessed guidance he has led and is still leading us! Take thy pencil and paper, and try to set down in figures or in words thy total indebtedness to his love; where wilt thou begin, and when thou hast begun, where wilt thou finish? If thou wert to record only one out of a million of his love-gifts to thee, would the whole world be able to contain the books that might be written concerning them? No; all thou canst say is, "Behold *how* he has loved us!"

There have been times—of which I will not say much just now, for some here would not understand what I mean,—when we have seemed to stand in the very suburbs of heaven, where we could hear the bells pealing forth celestial music from the invisible belfries, and our hearts were ravished with the sound of the heavenly harpers harping with their harps, and the ten thousand times ten thousand white-robed choristers singing the song of Moses and of the Lamb. Nay, more than that, the King himself hath brought us into his banqueting house, and his banner over us has been love. He has not only permitted us to sit at his feet, as Mary did, but he has allowed us to pillow our head on his bosom, as John did, and even condescended to let us put our finger into the print of the nails in our rapturous familiar fellowship with him who is not ashamed to call us his brethren. I must not continue in this strain,—not for lack of matter, but for lack of time in which to speak concerning him, so must again say, "Behold how he loved us!"

I must, however, mention one more proof of Christ's love, and that is this, *he has made us long for heaven, and given us at least a measure of preparation for it.* We are expecting that, one of these days, if the chariot and horses of fire do not stop at our door, our dear Lord and Saviour will fulfil to us his promise, "if I go and prepare a place for you, I will come again, and receive you unto myself; that where I am, there ye may be also." To a true believer in Jesus, the thought of departing from this world, and going to be "for ever with the Lord," has nothing of gloom associated with it. This earth is the place of our banishment and exile; heaven is our home. We are like the loving wife who is sundered by thousands of miles of sea and land from her dear husband, and we are longing for the great re-union with our beloved Lord, from whom we shall then never again be separated. I cannot hope to depict the scene when he shall introduce us to the principalities and powers in heavenly places, and bid us sit with him in his throne, even as he sits with his Father in *his* throne. Surely then the holy angels, who have never sinned, will unite in exclaiming, "Behold, how he loved them!" It is a most blessed thought, to my mind, that we may be up there before the hands of that clock complete another round; and if not so soon as that, it will not be long before all of us who love the Lord will be with him where he is, and then the least among us shall know more of his love than the greatest of us can ever know while here below. Meanwhile, we have much of the joy of heaven even while we are upon this earth; for, as Paul wrote to the Ephesians, "God, who is rich in mercy, for his great love wherewith he loved us, even when we were dead in sins, hath quickened us together with Christ, (by grace ye are saved;) and hath raised us up together, and made us sit together in heavenly places in Christ Jesus."

III. The closing portion of my sermon is to be very practical. Did anybody ever say of any one of us here, "Behold how he loves Christ"? If someone did say that of *you*, my brother or sister, was it true? I think I hear your answer, "Oh, I do love him! He knows all things, and he knows that I love him." But do you love him so fervently that strangers or even your more intimate acquaintances would say of your love to Jesus what the Jews said of his love to Lazarus, "Behold how he loved him"? "I wish," says one, "I could do so." Then listen for a minute or two while I tell you of WHAT SOME SAINTS HAVE DONE TO SHOW HOW THEY LOVED THEIR LORD.

There have been *those who have suffered for Christ's sake*. They have lain in damp dungeons, and have refused to accept liberty at the price of treachery to their Lord and his truth. They have been stretched upon the rack, yet no torture could make them yield up their fidelity to God. If you have read *Foxe's Book of Martyrs*, you know how hundreds of brave men and women, and children too, stood at the stake, gloriously calm, and often triumphantly happy, and were burnt to death for Christ's sake, while many of those who looked on learnt to imitate their noble example, and others who heard their dying testimonies, and their expiring songs, (not groans,) could not help exclaiming, "Behold how these martyrs love their Master!"

There have been others, *who have shown their love to their Lord by untiring and self-sacrificing service*. They have laboured for him, at times, under great privations and amid many perils, some as missionaries in foreign lands, and others with equal zeal in this country. Their hearts were all aglow with love for their dear Lord and Saviour, and they spent their whole time and strength in seeking to win souls for him, so that those who knew them could not help saying, "Behold how they love their Lord!" Some of us can never hope to wear the ruby crown of martyrdom, yet we may be honoured by receiving the richly-jewelled crown from the hand of Christ as he says to each of his true labourers, "Well done, thou good and faithful servant: . . . enter thou into the joy of thy Lord."

Then we have known *some saints who showed their love to their Lord by weeping over sinners and praying for their conversion*. There have been gracious men and women, who could not sleep at night because of their anxiety about the eternal welfare of their relatives and friends, or even of lost ones who were personally unknown to them; and they have risen from their beds to agonize in prayer for sinners who were either calmly sleeping, and not even dreaming of their doom, or else at that very hour were adding to their many previous transgressions. There have been others, who could not hear a blasphemous word, as they passed along the street, without feeling a holy indignation at the injury that was being done to their best Friend, and at the same time their eyes filled with tears of pity for the poor blasphemers, and their hearts poured out a stream of supplication for those who were thus ignorantly or wantonly sinning against the Most High. They have been like Jeremiah weeping over the lost, and like Moses and Paul ready to sacrifice their own souls for the sake of others, until men have been compelled to say, "Behold how these weeping and pleading saints love their Lord, and love lost sinners for his sake!"

Others have proved their love to their Lord by the way in which they have given of their substance to his cause. They have not only given a tithe of all they had to the great Melchizedek, but they have counted it a high privilege to lay all that they had upon his altar, counting that their gold was never so golden as when it was all Christ's, and that their lands were never so valuable to them as when they were gladly surrendered to him. Alas, that there should be so few, even in the Church of Christ, who thus imitate their Lord who freely gave himself and all he had that he might save his people! Blessed will the Church be when she gets back to the Pentecostal consecration which was the fitting culmination of the Pentecostal blessing: "all that believed were together, and had all things common; and sold their possessions and goods, and parted them to all men, as every man had need."

Another most admirable way of proving our love to Christ is *by being scrupulously careful to please him in little things as well as in the more important matters.* One of the worst signs of this present evil age is that so little is thought of even the great things of Christ,—his atoning sacrifice, his high priestly character and work, his kingly rule, and so on; while the little things of Christ, those that are less by comparison with these, are often utterly despised. There was a time, in Scotland, when men of God signed the Solemn League and Covenant with their blood; how many would do that to-day? One jewel in Christ's crown, that priceless Koh-i-noor of the crown rights of the King of kings, was sufficient to call into the battlefield the noblest of Scotland's sons; but, to-day, the very crown of Christ itself is kicked about, like a football, by some of his professed servants, for they set up their own fallible judgments against his infallible revelation, and so practically say, "We will not have this Man to reign over us!" In this land, in the most glorious days that England has ever seen, our Puritan forefathers were so scrupulous that men called them strait-laced, sour-faced, bigoted, and I know not what; but, nowadays, many of the truths for which they contended, and for which many of them resisted even unto blood, are said to be unimportant or of no account whatever. The special truth which distinguishes us as a denomination is regarded by many with supreme contempt.

Not long ago, a professedly Christian minister said that he did not care a penny about baptism! If he belongs to Christ, he will have to answer to his Master for that saying; but I could not utter such a sentence as that without putting my very soul in peril. He who really loves his Lord will not trifle with the least jot or tittle of his Lord's will. Love is one of the most jealous things in the universe. "God is a jealous God" because "God is love." The wife who truly loves her husband will not harbour even a wanton imagination; her fidelity to him must not be stained even by an unchaste thought; so must it be with every true lover of the Lord Jesus Christ. God grant that we, beloved brethren and sisters in Christ, may do our Lord's will so scrupulously, in great things and little things, and in all things alike, that those who see us in our daily life may be compelled to say, "Behold how these Christians love Jesus Christ their Lord and Saviour!"

Yet, beloved, remember that, when our love has reached its climax, it can only be like a solitary dewdrop trembling on a leaf compared with the copious showers of love that pour continually from the heart of our dear Lord and Master. Put all our loves together, and they will not fill a tiny cup, and there before us flows the fathomless, limitless, shoreless ocean of the love of Jesus; yet let us have all the love for him that we can. May the Holy Spirit fill our souls to the brim with love to Jesus, for his dear name's sake! Amen.

2. God's Love to the Saints

"Hereby perceive we the love of God, because he laid down his life for us."— 1 John iii. 16.

TRUE love cannot long be dormant. It is like fire, of an active nature; it must be at work. Love longs for expression; it cannot be dumb. Command it to be without expression, and you command it not to live. And true love is not satisfied with expressing itself in words. It does use words, but it is painfully conscious of their feebleness, for the full meaning of love is not to be conveyed in any human language. It breaks the backs of words, and crushes them to atoms when it lays upon them all that it means. Love must express itself in deeds, as our old proverb says, "Actions speak more loudly than words." Love delights, too, in sacrifices; she rejoices in self-denials; and the more costly the sacrifice, the better is love pleased to make it. She will not offer that which costs her nothing; she loves to endure pains, and losses, and crosses, and thus she expresses herself best.

This is a general principle, which is not only applicable to men, but it reaches even up to God himself; for "God is love," and being love, he must display love, nor can he rest with merely speaking of his love. His love must manifest itself in action. More than that, God could not rest until he had made the greatest sacrifice that he could make, and had given up his only-begotten Son to die in the place of sinners. When he had done that, then he could rest in his love. God does not come to us, and say, "Men and women, I love you; and you must believe that I love you although I do nothing for you to prove my love." He does ask us to believe in his love, but he has given us abundant proofs of it; and, therefore, he has a right to claim our belief in it. The apostle of love, who wrote the chapter from which our text is taken, tells us, "Hereby we are made to know"

—for that would be the real translation of the original,—" Hereby we come to know, we do know, the love of God, because he laid down his life for us." Just as we learn the love of others by seeing what they are prepared to sacrifice for us, so is it even with God himself, we discover, discern, perceive, and are made to know, the love which he bears to us by the fact that "he laid down his life for us."

I. First, I want to show you that THERE ARE MANY ACTS OF GOD IN WHICH HIS LOVE IS VERY CLEAR, BUT IN WHICH THE MOST OF MEN FAIL TO SEE IT.

There are many of his acts, of which it might be said, "Hereby the love of God is manifested;" yet many men fail to perceive the love which lies behind the actions. Let us examine ourselves, to see how we stand with regard to this matter. There are some of us, who ought to have perceived the love of God to us *in the surroundings into which we were brought at our very birth.* I am addressing many who, like myself, owe very much to Christian parentage. Many of us could truly say, in the words of the children's hymn,—

> "I was not born, as thousands are,
> Where God was never known,
> And taught to pray a useless prayer
> To blocks of wood and stone."

But, without being born slaves or heathens, it might have happened that we should have had to spend our childhood in the slums of London. Some of you think that you have been very good; but would you have been better than the boys that fill our reformatories, —would you have been better than those who crowd our prisons,— if you had had the same training, or lack of training, that has been their lot? If you had had such an example as they have had,—if the taste of strong drink had been familiar to you almost from your birth,—if the first thing you ever heard was blasphemy,—if you had lived in the thieves' kitchen,—do you think that you would have been any more clear from guilt than they have been? When we look down upon others, and despise them, it may be that, if we knew all their temptations, and the conditions of their upbringing, we might almost admire them for not being worse than they are. It costs some people a great struggle to be honest; and there are many women, in this dreadful London, whom we, perhaps, think ill of, who, nevertheless, have suffered almost a martyrdom, and who have fought stern battles with temptation; if they have fallen somewhat, they are to be honoured because they have not fallen still further.

But what a blessing it was to us that, when we woke up in this world, we looked up into a face that smiled upon us, and to lips that, by-and-by, spake to us of Jesus Christ. The first example that we had was one that, to this day, we wish to follow. Our companions, from our youth up, have been of a godly order; and there are some, who are in heaven now, who had much to do with the formation of our character, and for whom we should always thank God. Now, had we been wise,—had we understood the meaning of this gracious arrangement,—we might, in the very conditions in which we were born, and brought up, have perceived the love of God to us; yet many of us did not. I should not wonder if some of you thought that you were badly treated because you were placed in such a strict family, where you were checked, and kept from what you regarded as the pleasures of life. Many a young man has felt that he has been tied to his mother's apron-string a great deal too much. He saw other young men enjoying themselves, but he could not; his father, like a grim jailer, was always looking after him so closely. That is the way many of us put it in the days of our ignorance; but, now that God has opened our eyes, we can see the love of God in it all. Yet we did not see it then; and, as a general rule, young men and women, who have the high privilege of Christian parentage and training, do not perceive the love of God in it, but often kick against it, and wish they had not to endure what they regard as so great a hardship.

Then, dear friends, the love of God may be clearly seen in reference to all of us *in his giving us a wise and judicious law.* That law of the ten commandments is a gift of great kindness to the sons of men, for it tells us the wisest and the happiest way of living. It forbids us nothing but what would be to our injury, and it withholds from us nothing which would be a real pleasure to us. The commands which say, " Thou shalt " or " Thou shalt not " are like the boards, which you sometimes see at bathing-places, bearing the words, " Dangerous! Keep so many yards away from this spot." God does not make laws denying us anything that would really be for our good. There is a poisonous berry growing in your garden, and your child has been told that he is not to eat it. If he is a wise child, he will understand that it is your love to him which has told him not to eat of that poisonous berry. If you had no care about him at all, he might eat what poison he chose; but, because you love him, you say to him, " My child, do not this, and do not that, because it will be to your serious injury, and possibly your death, if you disobey." We ought to see the love of God in the gift of the law, but nobody ever does that till he is led to see the love of God in other ways. We cannot say of it, though we ought to do so, " Hereby perceive we the love of God towards us."

We have also had, *in the daily bounties of divine providence,* abundant manifestations of the love of God. If our eyes were really opened, every loaf of bread would come to us as a token of our Father's care, and every drop we drink would come as the gift of our Father's bounty. Are we not clothed by his love? The breath that is in our nostrils,—who gives it to us but our Creator? Who preserves us in health but our great Benefactor? Is it not a proof of love that you are not to-night on a sick-bed,—that you are not in the lunatic-asylum,—that you are not on the borders of the grave;—ay, and that you are not in hell? We are a mass of mercies and a mass of sins; we seem to be made of mercy and ingratitude mixed together. But if the Lord will open our eyes, we shall then perceive the boundless mercies of which we are the recipients, and we shall begin to perceive his love; but this is not the first place where man ever sees God's love. The cross is the lancet window through which the love of God is best seen; but, until that window is opened, all the bounties of God's providence fail to convince us of his love. See how the mass of men reap their harvests, and yet never bless the God who gives the harvest. See how they drive the loaded wains to the granaries, and thresh out the wheat, and send it to be sold in the markets; but did you ever hear of a song of praise being sung in the market when they brought the first new wheat to be sold? Did you ever hear of such a thing? Why, they would think we were all gone mad if, at Mark Lane, on the arrival of a sample of new wheat, we were to begin to sing—

> "Praise God from whom all blessings flow."

The probability is that there are many of them there cursing because the wheat has gone down a shilling or two, and the poor people will, possibly, get their bread a little cheaper. Praising God seems to have gone out of fashion, and we are told by philosophers, who ought to know, that the wheat springs up naturally, and that God has nothing to do with it. They say that, whether it rains or whether the sun shines, the processes of nature are ruled by iron law with which God has no concern at all; and they practically imply that he has gone out for a holiday, and left the world to manage itself, or wound it up, like a watch, and put it under his pillow, and gone to sleep. That is the philosopher's religion; and, as far as I am concerned, the philosophers may keep it, for it is not mine. My religion believes in the God of the showers, and the God of the sunshine, and the God of the harvests. I believe in "the living God, who giveth us richly all things to enjoy;" and let his name be praised for it. Were our hearts right with him, we should "hereby" perceive the love of God, but we do not; that perception comes to us through a stained glass window, the window that was stained crimson by the precious blood of Christ. There, and only there, do we perceive the love of God, "because he laid down his life for us."

II. That brings me to my second point, which is this, IN THE LAYING DOWN OF HIS LIFE, CHRIST'S LOVE IS BEST SEEN.

I have already said that, in many acts of God, his love ought to be seen; but, according to the text, we "hereby" perceive the love of God, "because he laid down his life for us." It is universally admitted that *there can be no greater proof of love than for a person to lay down his life for the object of that love.* All sorts of sacrifices may be taken as proofs of affection, but the relinquishment of life is the supreme proof of love, which nobody doubts. A man says that he loves his country; but suppose that man should be in the condition of Curtius, in the old Roman fable, when a great chasm opened in the Forum, and it was declared that it could only be closed by the most precious thing in Rome being thrown into it. The story goes on to say that Curtius, fully armed, and riding his charger, leaped into the chasm, which instantly closed. Well, nobody could doubt the love of such a man for his country. If the question happened to be the love of humanity, we have the story—the true story—of the surgeon at Marseilles; and if we acted as he did, nobody could doubt our love to our fellow-creatures. The plague was raging through the city, and the people were dying by thousands. The good bishop remained among them, discharging the last offices to the dying, and cheering the living; and many of the surgeons of the town, who might have departed, lingered to wait upon the sick. At a consultation among them, it was resolved to make a *post mortem* examination of one of the worst cases of the pest; and the question was, who should make it, for, whoever did it must certainly die of the disease within a few hours. One of them, to his honour, said, "My life is of no more value than that of any other man; why should I not sacrifice it, if I can, by doing so, discover the cause of this terrible malady, and save this city?" He finished his grim task, wrote his notes about the case, and then went to his home, and died. Nobody doubted that he loved Marseilles, for he had laid down his life for it. And you probably read, the other day, the story of a mother's love, which nobody could doubt. In the late disastrous floods, a mother, who had her two little children in a cradle, climbed a hill, carrying them with her; she reached a tree, or some other frail shelter, with these two dear objects of her love, and held them up till she found that the support, on which she was resting, was not strong enough to sustain herself and her two babes; so, placing them, as far as she could, out of harm's way, she leaped into the waters, and soon sank. Nobody could doubt that mother's love when she laid down her life for her children. This is the crowning proof of love; even "the devil's advocate" will not rise up to dispute this truth. They that can die for others must surely love those for whom they lay down their lives.

Now, *our Lord Jesus Christ has proved his love to sinners by dying for them.* Do you need me to tell you the story again? O my brothers and sisters, read it for yourselves; read it often! You have it written four times, but not once too often,—the story of the Son of God, who, for our sakes, died a felon's death, barbarously nailed to the cross to bleed away his life. Read that story, and see how he proved his love to us.

But there were certain points about Christ's death which are very extraordinary, and which are better proofs of love than those I mentioned just now. The first is this,—*Jesus need not have died at all.* When the Marseilles surgeon died, he only did then what he must have done a few years afterwards. When the mother perished to save her children, she did but die a few weeks, or months, or years, before her appointed time; for, being mortal, she must die. If we do give our life for others, we do not really give our life; we but pay the debt of nature a little while before it is due; but it was altogether different in the Lord Jesus Christ's case. Over him, death had no power. It is of him that Paul writes, " who only hath immortality." Who could, without his own consent, have laid his hand upon the Prince of life, the Son of God, and said to him, "Thou shalt die"? No one could have done that; it was a purely voluntary act for Christ to die at all;—not merely to die on the cross, but ever to die, was a voluntary act on his part; and, consequently, a most singular proof of his love to us.

Remember, again, that in our Lord's case, *there were no claims upon him on the part of those for whom he died.* I can understand a mother dying for her children. "Can a woman forget her sucking child, that she should not have compassion on the son of her womb?" I can see some reason why a noble citizen should be willing to die for his city. When the six principal burgesses of Calais put the ropes round their necks, and went out to Edward III., to offer to die instead of their fellow-citizens, I can understand their action. Were they not the leaders of that community? Were they not put into a position of responsibility and honour which, if it might not exactly demand the sacrifice, yet, at least, rendered it a most likely thing that, if they were men of truly noble spirit, they would make it? But there were no such claims upon our Lord Jesus Christ. When Queen Eleanor sucked the poison from her husband's wounds, at the risk of her own life, I can see reasons why she should do it. I say not that she was bound to do it, but I do say that the relationship of a wife accounts for what she did. But Jesus Christ, the Son of God, had no relationship to us until he chose to assume the relationship which he did assume out of infinite compassion. There was no more relation between him and us than between the potter and the clay; and if the clay upon the wheel goes amiss, what does the potter do with it but take it, and throw it into a corner? And so might the great Creator have done with us; but, instead of doing so, he sheds his blood that he may make us into vessels of honour fit for his own use. O Son of God, how couldst thou stoop so low as to take upon thyself our nature, and in that nature to bleed and die, when between us and thee there was a distance infinitely greater than that between an emmet and a cherub, or a moth and an archangel? Yet, with no claims upon thee, of thine own free will, thou didst yield thyself to die because of thine amazing love to us.

Another extraordinary thing about Christ's love was that *there were no appeals whatever made to him to die.* In the other cases which I have quoted, you may remind me that there were no vocal appeals made. The little children in the cradle did not beg their mother to die for them. No, but the very sight of them was enough to plead with their mother. In the case of the city dying of pestilence, could the surgeon,—who believed that, by an examination, he might discover the secret of the evil,—go through the streets, and see the doors marked with the fatal cross, and hear the wailing of the widows and the children, without feeling that they did make most pitiful appeals to his heart? But man made no appeal to God to die for him. Our father Adam—and he was the representative of us all,—did not fall down on his knees in the presence of God, and say, "God be merciful to me a sinner. O God, whom I have offended, provide for me a Saviour, and deliver me from thy wrath!" No prayer came from Adam's lips, and not even a confession; only a wicked and mean attempt to cast upon God the blame for his disobedience: "The woman whom thou gavest to be with me, she gave me of the tree, and I did eat." That is all that human nature usually does; it will not own that it needs a Saviour, and it will not confess that it has sinned sufficiently to need an expiatory sacrifice; and, consequently, the sullenness of man might have paralyzed the love of Christ if anything could have done it. You did not sue for mercy,—you did not ask for an atonement,—you did not desire expiation for your sin; yet Jesus came, unasked, undesired, unsought, to lay down his life for sinners.

Notice, again, that Jesus Christ well knew that, if he did lay down his life, *he would get no love in return from those for whom he died, unless he himself created that love.* This he has done in the hearts of his own people; but, in the hearts of others who have been left to themselves, there is no love to Jesus Christ. Here, Sabbath after Sabbath, it is our privilege to preach a dying Saviour to dying sinners; but, of all themes in the world, it seems to make the least impression upon some of our hearers. If we were to come here, and talk of Howard's devotion in living and dying to ameliorate the woes of the prisoners in our jails, many would be moved to admiration of the philanthropist; but how little admiration have most men for our sweet Lord and Master! It is an old story, you say, and you have heard it so often that you care little for it. Now, that mother, who died to save her children, felt that they loved her. How often they had charmed her with their cooings and smilings while they were lying in her bosom, and she felt that she could freely give up her life for them. But our Lord Jesus Christ knew that he was dying for stony-hearted monsters, whose return for his love, if left to themselves, would be that they would utterly reject him. They would not believe in him; they would trust in their own righteousness rather than in his, and they would try to find a way to heaven by sacraments and ceremonies rather than by faith in the meritorious sacrifice which he made when he laid down his life for sinners.

Remember, too, that *our Lord died by the hands of men, as well as for the sake of men.* The surgeon at Marseilles was not to die by the act of his fellow-citizens. The mother was not to die at the hands of her children. Curtius, leaping into the gulf, was not forced there by the anger of his fellow-citizens. On the contrary, all would have been glad for them to continue to live. But it was this that made the death of Christ so sadly unique, that he came to die for men who wished that he should be made to die. "Crucify him, crucify him," they cried in their mad rage, foaming at the mouth. "Oh!" say some of you, "but we never said that." No, not then; but perhaps you are saying it now; for there are still many who hate the gospel of Christ, and to hate the gospel is to hate Christ himself, for that is his very essence and heart; and to reject Christ, to choose your own pleasure, and to keep on delaying to repent, as some of you do, and to live at enmity against Christ, is very much the same thing as crying, "Crucify him," and comes to the same thing in the long run. You know that, if you could be quite sure that there is no Christ, and no God, and no heaven, and no hell, you would be perfectly happy. That is to say, you would, if you could, crucify Christ, and put him out of existence, with everything that has to do with him. Well, that is the very same spirit as that which made the Jews of old cry, " Crucify him, crucify him."

Yet once more, there was this remarkable thing about Christ's death,—that, *in dying for us, he was taking upon himself an awful mass of shame and dishonour, and also a most intimate connection with sin.* There was nothing shameful about the leap of Curtius into the chasm; had I been there to see him, I would have clapped my hands, and cried, "Well done, Curtius!" Who would not have said the same? But when our Lord died, men thrust out their tongues at him, and mocked him. His was indeed a shameful death. And, methinks, when that mother put her babes up in a place of safety, and herself sank into the raging flood, the angels might have smiled as well as sorrowed at such a deed of heroism. But when Jesus sank into the raging flood to save us, even God himself did not smile at him. Amongst our Saviour's expiring cries was that agonizing utterance, "My God, my God, why hast thou forsaken me?" This was because he had, as our Representative, come into contact with human sin, and so with human shame. The just and holy Son of God was made a curse for us; or, as Paul tells us, God "hath made him to be sin for us, who knew no sin; that we might be made the righteousness of God in him."

All this helps to manifest to us Christ's amazing love, so I finish my discourse by asking,—as the text says, "Hereby perceive we the love of God, because he laid down his life for us,"—*have you and I perceived that love?* Do we know it? That is a very simple question, yet I take the liberty to press it upon you. I think it is Aristotle who says,—and he was a great master of thought,—that it is impossible for a person to know that he is loved without feeling some love in return. I think, as a rule, that is true; so, if you do really perceive that Christ loved you so much as to die for you, there will leap up in your heart somewhat, at any rate, of love to him. One Sunday night, I was reading, in Exeter Hall, the hymn beginning—

"Jesu, Lover of my soul,"

and, just at the time, there strayed into the hall a man of fashion, a man of the world, careless of all spiritual things; but that line caught his ear,—

"Jesu, Lover of my soul."

He said to himself, "Does Jesus really love *me?* Is he the Lover of *my* soul?" and that line was the means of begetting love in his thoughtless heart, and there and then he surrendered himself to the love of Christ. Oh, that such a result as that might come of my repeating the story here,—that some, who have never loved the Lord Jesus Christ up till now, would say, "Did he thus love his enemies,—thus strangely love them even to the death? Then we, though we have hitherto been his enemies, can be his enemies no longer, but we will love him in return for his great love to us."

And you Christian people, who do love him, if you have perceived his love somewhat, try to perceive it still more, that you may love him more; and if you really love him more, try to show that you do. Notice the rest of the verse from which my text is taken; I did not leave out the latter part because I was afraid of it, but because I had not time to deal with it as it deserves: "Hereby perceive we the love of God, because he laid down his life for us: and we ought to lay down our lives for the brethren." We ought to prove our love to our God by our love to our fellow-men, and especially by our love to our fellow-Christians, and to prove our love by our actions. I do not know what the love of some professors is worth; I suppose they do, if they put down how much it costs them in a year. I fear that it does not cost some professors nearly as much for their religion as it does for their ribbons, or for some foolish indulgence. They pay their shoeblacks better than they pay their ministers, and they take care to spend upon themselves, in perfect waste, a hundred times as much as they spend upon spreading the gospel, saving the heathen, helping the poor, or rescuing the fallen. We do not believe in such Christianity as that, and certainly do not wish to practise it. If we profess to be Christians, let us be Christians in deed, and let us especially show our love to Christ by loving our fellow-Christians. If you see any of them in need, aid them to the uttermost of your power. If they want cheering and comforting, give them good cheer and comfort; but, if they need substantial aid, financial aid, let them have that, too. In the old days of persecution, there were always some noble souls who tried to hide away the Christians from those who sought their lives, although they did so at the risk of their own lives; and many a Christian has given himself up to die in order to save the lives of his fellow-Christians. Some of the old people came tottering before the judge, because they thought that they would not be so much missed from the church as the younger ones would be; and, possibly, some of them also thought that they had more faith than the younger ones had; and if they had more faith, they were more ready to die, and so to let the younger ones live on until they grew stronger in faith, and hope, and love. But, on the other hand, sometimes the young men would gently push back the fathers, and say to them, "No; you are old: you had better linger here awhile, and teach the young; but we young people are strong, so we will go and die for Christ;" and there was many a contention, in the Church of God, in persecuting times, as to who should first die for Christ. They were all willing to lay down their lives for their brethren. Where has this self-sacrificing love gone to now? I would like to see some of it; I would even wear microscopes over my eyes if I thought that I could so discover it; but I am afraid I cannot. Why, if we loved each other now as Christians loved each other then, we should be the theme of the talk of the town, and even worldlings would say, "See how these Christians love one another." Yet this is only what we ought to do; so, brothers and sisters in Christ, let it be what we will do. God help you to do it, for Christ's sake! Amen.

3. The Poor Man's Friend

"The poor committeth himself unto thee."—Psalm x. 14.

GOD is the poor man's Friend; the poor man, in his helplessness and despair, leaves his case in the hands of God, and God undertakes to care for him. In the days of David,—and I suppose, in this respect, the world has but little improved,—the poor man was the victim of almost everybody's cruelty, and sometimes he was very shamefully oppressed. If he sought redress for his wrongs, he generally only increased them, for he was regarded as a rebel against the existing order of things; and when he asked for even a part of what was his by right, the very magistrates and rulers of the land became the instruments of his oppressors, and made the yoke of his bondage to be yet heavier than it was before. Tens of thousands of eyes, full of tears, have been turned to Jehovah, and he has been invoked to interpose between the oppressor and the oppressed; for God is the ultimate resort of the helpless. The Lord executeth righteousness and judgment for all that are oppressed; he undertakes the cause of all those that are downtrodden.

If the history of the world be rightly read, it will be found that no case of oppression has been suffered to go long unpunished. The Assyrian empire was a very cruel one, but what is now left of Nineveh and Babylon? Go to the heaps of ruins by the banks of the Tigris and the Euphrates, and see what will become of an empire which is made to be only an instrument of oppression in the hands of an emperor and the great men under him. It has ceased to be more than a name; its power has vanished, and its palaces have been destroyed. In later times, there sprang up the mighty empire of Rome; and even now, wherever we wander, we see traces of its greatness and splendour. How came it to fall? Many reasons have been assigned, but you may rest assured that at the bottom of them all was the cruelty practised towards the slaves, and other poor people, who were absolutely in the power of

24

the aristocracy and oligarchy who formed the dominant party in the empire. There is a fatal flaw in the foundations of any throne that executes not justice; and it matters not though the empire seems to stand high as heaven, and to raise its pinnacles to the skies, down it must come if it be not founded upon right. When ten thousand slaves have cried to God apparently in vain, it has not really been in vain, for he has registered their cries, and in due season has avenged their wrongs; and when the poor toilers, who have reaped the rich man's fields, have been deprived of their hardly-earned wages, and have cast their plaints into the court of heaven, they have been registered there, and God has, at the right time, taken up their cause, and punished their oppressors.

For many years the negro slaves cried to God to deliver them, and at last deliverance came, to the joy of the emancipated multitudes, yet not without suffering to all the nations that had been concerned in that great wrong. And here, too, if the employers of labour refuse to give to the agricultural labourer his just wage, God will surely visit them in his wrath. At this very day, we have serfs in England who, with sternest toil, cannot earn enough to keep body and soul together, and to maintain their families as they ought to be maintained; and where masters are thus refusing to their labourers a fair remuneration for their work, let them know that, whoever may excuse them, and whatever may be said of the laws of political economy, God does not judge the world by political economy. He judges the world by this rule, that men are bound to do that which is just and right to their fellow-men; and it can never be right that a man should work like a slave, be housed worse than a horse, and have food scarcely fit for a dog. But if the poor commit their case to God, he will undertake it; and I, as one of God's ministers, will never cease to speak on behalf of the rights of the poor. The whole question has two sides,—the rights of the masters, and the rights of the men. Let not the men do as some workmen do, ask more than they ought; yet, on the other hand, let not the masters domineer over their men, but remember that God is the Master of us all, and he will see that right is done to all. Let us all act rightly towards one another, or we shall feel the weight of his hand, and the force of his anger.

Now, having thus given the literal meaning of my text, I am going to spiritualize it, which I should have no right to do if I had not first explained the primary reference of David's words, " The poor committeth himself unto thee."

I. THERE ARE SPIRITUALLY POOR MEN; and these do what other poor men have done in temporal things, they commit their case into the hands of God.

Let me try to find out the spiritually poor. They are, first, *those who have no merits of their own.* There are some people, in the world, who are, according to their own estimate, very rich in good works. They think that they began well, and that they have gone on well, and they hope to continue to do well right to the end of their lives. They do confess, sometimes, that they are miserable sinners, but that is merely because that expression is in the Prayer Book. They are half sorry it is there, but they suppose that it must have been meant for other people, not for themselves. So far as they know, they have kept all the commandments from their youth up, they have been just in their dealings with their fellow-men, and they do not feel that they are under any very serious obligations even to God himself. I have nothing to say to such people except to remind them that the Lord Jesus Christ said, " They that are whole have no need of the physician, but they that are sick : I came not to call the righteous, but sinners to repentance." Christ came to bring healing to those who are spiritually sick ; you say that you are perfectly well, so you must go your own way, and Christ will go in another direction,—towards sinners.

Further, the poor people, of whom I am speaking, are not only totally without anything like merit, absolutely bankrupt of any goodness, and devoid of anything of which they could boast, but they are also *without strength to perform any such good works in the future.* They are so poor, spiritually, that they cannot even pray as they would, and they do not even feel their poverty as they would like to feel it. After having read this Bible, they wish they could re-read it with greater profit ; and when they weep over sin, they feel their own sin in their very tears, and want to weep in penitence over their tears. They are such poor people that they can do absolutely nothing without Christ, and so poor that, in them, that is, in their flesh, there dwelleth no good thing. They did think once that there might be something good in them ; but they have searched their nature through most painfully, and they have discovered that, unless grace shall do everything for them, where God is they can never come.

Perhaps some of you say, " These must be very bad people." Well, they are no better than they should be, yet I may tell you another thing concerning them, they are no worse than many of those who think themselves a great deal better. They have this lowly opinion of themselves because the grace of God has taught them to think rightly and truthfully about themselves in relation to God. They are, in outward appearance, and as far as we can judge, quite as good as others, and better than some. In certain respects, they might be held up as examples to others. This is what we say of them, but they have not a good word to say of themselves ; rather, do they put their finger upon their lips, and blush at the remembrance of what they feel themselves to be ; or if they must speak of themselves at all, they say, " All we like sheep have gone astray, we have turned every one to his own way."

II. That brings me to notice, secondly, WHAT THESE POOR PEOPLE DO. They commit themselves unto God. This is a very blessed description of what true faith does. The poor in spirit feel that their case is so desperate that they cannot keep it in their own charge, and therefore they commit it to God. I will try to show you how they do that.

First, *they commit their case to God as a debtor commits his case to a surety.* The man is so deeply in debt that he cannot pay his creditors even a farthing in the pound; but here is someone who can pay everything that the debtor owes, and he says to him, " I will stand as security for you; I will be bondsman for you; I will give full satisfaction to all your creditors, and discharge all your debts." There is no person who is thus deeply in debt, who would not be glad to know of such a surety, both able and willing to stand in his stead, and to discharge all his responsibilities. If the surety said to this poor debtor, " Will you make over all your liabilities to me? Will you sign this document, empowering me to take all your debts upon myself, and to be responsible for you? Will you let me be your bondsman and surety?" " Ah!" the poor man would reply, "that I will, most gladly." That is just what spiritually poor men have done to the Lord Jesus Christ,—committed their case, with all their debts and liabilities, into the hands of the Lord Jesus Christ, and he has undertaken all the responsibility for them.

I think I hear someone say, " But will Christ really stand in the sinner's place in such a way as that?" Oh, yes! for he did stand, in anticipation, in the sinner's place before the foundation of the world, and he actually stood there when he died upon the accursed tree, by his death obtaining a full discharge of the debts of all those whose Surety he had become.* Dear soul, wilt thou not commit all thy affairs into his hands? Art thou not willing to let him stand as thy Surety, to clear thee of all thy liabilities? " Willing?" say you; " ah! that I am; and not only willing, but right glad shall I be for him to take my place, and relieve me of the burden that is crushing me to the dust." Then it is done for you, and so done that it can never be undone. Suppose that one of you had taken all my debts upon you, and that you were quite able and willing to pay them, I should not go home, and fret myself about my debts. I should rejoice to think that you had taken them upon yourself, and that therefore they would no longer be mine. If Christ has taken your sins upon himself,—and he has done so if you have truly trusted him, your sins have ceased to be; they are blotted out for ever. Christ nailed to his cross the record of everything that was against us; and, now, every poor sinner, who is indebted to God's law, and who trusteth in Christ, may know that his debt is cancelled, and that he is clear of all liability for it for ever.

Next, *we commit our case to Christ as a client does to a solicitor and advocate.*† You know that, when a man has a suit at law, (I hope that none of you may ever have such a suit,) if he has an advocate to plead his cause, he does not plead for himself. He will probably get into trouble if he does. It is said that, when Erskine was pleading for a man who was being tried for murder, his client, being dissatisfied with the way in which his defence was being conducted, wrote on a slip of paper, "I'll be hanged if I don't plead for myself." Erskine wrote in reply, "You'll be hanged if you do!" It is very much like that with us; if we attempt to plead for ourselves, we shall be sure to go wrong. We must have the Divine Advocate who alone can defend us against the suits of Satan, and speak with authority on our behalf even before the bar of God. We must commit our case to him, that he may plead for us, and then it will go rightly enough.

Remember also that any man, who has committed his case to an advocate, must not interfere with it himself. If anybody from the other side should wait upon him, and say, "I wish to speak to you about that suit," he must reply, "I cannot go into the matter with you; I must refer you to my solicitor." "But I want to reason about it; I want to ask you a few questions about the case." " No," says he, "I cannot listen to what you have to say, you must go to my solicitor." How much trouble Christians would save themselves if, when they have committed their case into the hands of Jesus, they would leave it there, and not attempt to deal with it on their own account! I say to the devil, when he comes to tempt me to doubt and fear, " I have committed my soul to Jesus Christ, and he will keep it in safety. You must bring your accusations to him, not to me. I am his client, and he is my Counsellor. Why should I have such an Advocate as he is, and then plead for myself?" John does not say, "If any man sin, let him be his own advocate;" but he says, "If any man sin, we have an Advocate with the Father, Jesus Christ the righteous." Dear brother, leave your case with Christ; he can handle it wisely, you cannot. Remember that, if the devil and you get into an argument, he is much older than you are, and far more clever than you are, and he knows a great many points of law that you do not know. You should always refer him to the Saviour, who is older than he is, and knows much more about law and everything else than he does, and who will answer him so effectually as to silence him for ever. So, poor tried and tempted soul, commit your case to the great Advocate, and he will plead for you before the Court of King's Bench in heaven, and your suit will be sure to succeed through his advocacy.

Further, *sinners commit their case to Christ as a patient commits his case to the physician.* We, poor sin-sick sinners, put our case into the hands of Jesus, that he may heal us of all our depravities, and evil tendencies, and infirmities. If anyone asks, "Will he undertake my case if I come to him?" I answer,—Yes, he came to be the Physician of souls, to heal all who trust him. There never was a case in which he could not heal, for he has a wonderful remedy, a catholicon, a cure for all diseases. If you put your case into his hands, the Holy Spirit will shed abroad his love in your heart, and there is no spiritual disease that can withstand that wondrous remedy. Are you predisposed to quickness of temper? He can cure that. Are you inclined to be indolent? Is there a sluggish spirit within you? He can cure that. Are you proud, or are your tendencies towards covetousness, worldliness, lust, or ambition? Christ can cure all these evils. When he was on this earth, he had all manner of patients brought to him, yet he never was baffled by one case, and your case, whatever it may be, will be quite an easy one to him if you only go and commit it into his hands. This building seems to me like a great hospital* full of sin-sick souls, and I pray the great Physician to come here, and heal them. Nay, I must correct myself, for he is here; and, as he walks through these aisles, and round these galleries, I beseech you to say to him, "Good Master, I commit myself to thee. I take thee to be my Saviour. O save me from my constitutional temperament, and my besetting sins, and everything else that is contrary to thy holy will!" He will hear you, for he never yet refused to heed the cry of a poor sin-sick soul. Do not let him go by you without praying to him, "Son of David, have mercy on me!" Come, Lord, and lay thy hands upon each one of us, and we shall be made perfectly whole!

As to the future, the spiritually poor commit themselves to Christ in the same way in which the pilgrims described in *The Pilgrim's Progress* committeth themselves to the charge of Mr. Greatheart, that he might fight all their battles for them, and conduct them safely to the Celestial City. In the old war times, when the captains of merchant vessels wanted to go to foreign countries, and they were afraid of being captured by the privateers of other nations, they generally went in company under the convoy of a man-of-war to protect them, and that is the way you and I must go to heaven. Satan's privateers will try to capture us, but we commit ourselves to the protection of Jesus, the Lord High Admiral of all the seas, and we poor little vessels sail safely under his convoy. When any enemy seeks to attack us, we need not be afraid. He can blow them all out of the water if he pleased, but he will never suffer one of them to injure a solitary vessel that is entrusted to his charge. Sinner, give thyself up to the charge of Jesus, to be convoyed to heaven; and thou over-anxious child of God, lay down all thine anxieties at the feet of Jesus, and rest in his infinite power and love, which will never let thee be lost.

I might thus multiply figures and illustrations of how we commit ourselves to Christ. We do it very much in the way in which our blind friends, sitting under the pulpit, got here this evening,—*they came by committing themselves to the care of guides.* Some of them can walk a good long way without a guide, but others could not have found their way here to-night without some friend upon whose arm they could lean. That is the way to get to heaven, by leaning upon Jesus. Do not expect to see him, but trust yourself to him, and lean hard upon him. He loves to be trusted, and faith has a wonderful charm for him. I was once near the Mansion House, and as I stood there, a poor blind man, who wished to cross over to the Bank, said to me, "Please, sir, lead me across; I know you will, for I am blind." I was not sure that I could do so, for it is not an easy task to lead a blind man across that part where so many cabs and omnibuses are constantly passing, but I managed it as best I could. I do not think I could have done it if the poor man had not said to me, "I know you will;" for then I thought that I must; and if you come to Christ, and say, "Lord Jesus, wilt thou lead me to heaven?" and tell him that you are sure that he will never let a poor blind soul miss its way, that you are sure you can trust him, that he is such a kind-hearted Saviour that he will never thrust away a guilty sinner who thus commits himself into his hands, and I am sure that he will be glad to save you, and that he will rejoice over you as he leads you safely home to heaven. If any of you can see with your natural eyes, and yet are blind spiritually, be glad that there is a blessed Guide to whom you can commit yourself, and do commit yourself to him. Christ leads the blind by a way that they know not, and he will continue to lead them until he brings them to the land where they will open their eyes, and see with rapture and surprise the splendours of paradise, and rejoice that they are all their own for ever.

Is not this work of the poor committing themselves to Christ a very easy task? It is a very easy thing for a debtor to commit his debts to his surety, for anyone to commit his case to his advocate, for a patient to trust himself to his physician, for a pilgrim to feel safe under a powerful convoy, and for a blind man to trust in his guide;—all this is very simple and easy. It does not need much explanation, and faith in Jesus is just as simple and just as easy as that. Why is it that we sometimes find that faith is difficult? It is because we are too proud to believe in Jesus. If we did but see ourselves as we really are, we should be willing enough to trust the Saviour; but we do not like going to heaven like blind people who need a guide, or like debtors who cannot pay a farthing in the pound. We want to have a finger in the pie, we want to do something towards our own salvation, we want to have some of the praise and glory of it. God save us from this evil spirit!

While it is a very simple thing for the spiritually poor to commit themselves to Christ, let me also say that it is an act which greatly glorifies God. Christ is honoured when any soul trusts in him; it is a joy to his heart to be trusted. When the feeble cling to him, he feels such joy as mothers feel when their little ones cling to them. Christ is glad when poor sin-sick souls come and trust him. It was for this very purpose that he came into the world, to meet the needs of guilty sinners. So this plan, while it is easy for us, is glorifying to him.

And I will add that it is a plan that never fails any who trust to it. There never was a single soul that committed its case to Christ, and then found him fail, and there never shall be such a soul so long as the earth endureth. He that believeth in Christ shall not be ashamed or confounded, world without end. "He that believeth on the Son hath everlasting life," and everlasting life can never be taken away from one who has received it.

I close by asking a question,—If the spiritually poor commit themselves unto God, what comes of it? Why, it makes them very happy. But are they not sinful? Oh, yes; but they commit themselves to God's grace, and his grace blots out all their sins for ever. Are they not feeble? Oh, yes; but their feebleness leads them to commit themselves to his omnipotence; and his strength is made perfect in their weakness. Are they not needy? Oh, yes; but then they bring their needs to him, and they receive out of his fulness "grace for grace." But are they not often in danger? Oh, yes, in a thousand dangers; but they come, and hide beneath the shadow of God's wings, and he covers them with his feathers, and there they rest in perfect security. His truth becomes their shield and buckler, so that they need not fear any foe. But are they not apt to slip? Oh, yes; but they commit themselves to him who gives his angels charge over them, to keep them in all their ways, and to bear them up in their hands, lest they should dash their feet against a stone. But are they not very fickle and changeable? Oh, yes; but they commit themselves to him who says, "I am Jehovah; I change not." But are they not unworthy? Oh, yes, in themselves they are utterly unworthy; but they commit themselves to him who is called The Lord their righteousness; and when they are clothed in his righteousness, they are looked upon by God as being "without spot, or wrinkle, or any such thing." But have they no sickness? Yes, but they commit themselves to Jehovah-Rophi, the Lord the Healer, and he either heals their sickness, or gives them the grace to endure it. Are they not poor? Yes, many of them are extremely so; but they commit themselves to the faithful Promiser, and so bread is given them, and their water is sure. But don't they expect to die? Oh, yes, unless the Lord should first come; but they are not afraid to die. This is the point, above all others, in which the spiritually poor commit themselves unto God. They have learnt that sweet prayer of David so well that it is often on their tongues, "Into thine hand I commit my spirit: thou hast redeemed me, O Lord God of truth." They did commit their spirit into God's hand years ago, and he has kept them until now, and they know that he will not fail them in their dying hour.

In conclusion, I pray every spiritually poor heart to commit itself to God. I like to do this every morning. Satan often comes and says, "You are no Christian; all your supposed Christian experience is false." Very well, suppose it has been false; then I will start afresh; saint or no saint, I will begin over again by trusting Christ to be my Saviour. When you, dear friend, wake to-morrow morning, let this be the first thing that you do,—commit yourself to Jesus Christ for the whole of the day. Say, "My Lord, here is my heart, which I commit to thee. While I am away from home, may my heart be full of the fragrance of thy blessed presence; and when I return at night, may I still find my heart in thy kind keeping!" And every night, ere we go to sleep, let us pray,—

"Should swift death this night o'ertake us,
  And our couch become our tomb ;
May the morn in heaven awake us,
  Clad in light and deathless bloom."

Are you going to a foreign land? Then, renew the committal of your life to God. Are you going to change your state, and enter upon the joys and responsibilities of married life? Then commit yourself to God. Are you going to a new situation, or opening a new business? Is any change coming over you? Then, make a new committal, or a re-committal of your soul to the Lord Jesus,—only take care that you do it heartily and thoroughly, and make no reserve. I rejoice to feel that I have committed myself to Christ as the slave of old committed himself to his master. When the time came for him to be set free under the Jewish law, he said to his master, " No, I do not want to go. I love you, I love your children, I love your household, I love your service; I do not want to be free." Then you know that the master was to take an awl, and fasten him by the ear to the door-post. I suppose this was done to see whether the man really wanted to remain with his master, or not. Ah, beloved! some of us have had our ears bored long ago; we have given ourselves up to Christ, and we have a mark upon us which we can never lose. Were we not buried with him by baptism unto death,—a symbol that we are dead to the world, and buried to the world, for his dear sake? Well, in that same way, give yourself wholly up to Jesus; commit yourself to him. As that young bride commits all her life's joys and hopes to that dear bridegroom into whose face she looks so lovingly, so, O souls, commit yourselves to that dearest Bridegroom in earth or heaven, —the Lord Jesus Christ. Commit yourselves to him, to love and to be loved,—his to obey, his to serve, and his to be kept,—his in life,—and you need not add " till death us do part," but you may say " till death shall wed us more completely, and we shall sit together at the marriage banquet above; and be for ever and for ever one before the throne of God." Thus the poor soul commits itself unto Christ, is married unto Christ, gets the portion which Christ possesses, becomes Christ's own, and then lives with Christ for ever. Oh, that this might be the time in which many a man and many a woman would commit themselves unto Christ! I do not merely mean you who are poor in pocket, but you who are poor in spirit, I am asking you to commit yourselves unto Christ. Do not put it off, but may this be the very hour in which you shall be committed to Christ, and he shall take possession of you to be his for ever and for ever! Amen and Amen.

4. Love's Birth and Parentage

"We love him, because he first loved us."—1 John iv. 19.

VERY simple words, but very full of meaning. I think I might say of this sentence what the poet says of prayer: it is "the simplest form of speech that infant lips can try," and yet it is one of the "sublimest strains that reach the majesty on high." Take a little believing child and ask her why she loves the Saviour, and she will reply at once, "Because he loved me and died for me:" then ascend to heaven where the saints are perfect in Christ Jesus and put the same question, and with united breath the whole choir of the redeemed will reply, "He hath loved us and washed us from our sins in his own blood." When we begin to love Christ we love him because he first loved us; and when we grow in grace till we are capable of the very highest degree of spiritual understanding and affection, we still have no better reason for loving him than this, "Because he first loved us."

This morning, in trying to preach from the text, I would pray the Holy Spirit that every person here may first *feel* it. It is wonderful the difference between a text read and heard and a text felt within the soul. Oh, that you this morning may be able to say from your hearts because you cannot help saying it, "*We love him*." If I were to say no more, but sit down in silence, and if you were all to spend the next three quarters of an hour in exercising the emotion of love to God it would be time most profitably spent. It is beyond measure beneficial to the soul to take her fill of love with the Lord Jesus; it is the sweet cure for all her ailments for her to have leisure to delight herself in the Lord, and faith enough to dwell at ease in his perfections. Be sure, then, to let your hearts have room, and scope, and opportunity for indulging and inflaming the sacred passion of love to God. If the second part of the text shall also be made equally vivid to you by the power of faith—"*He first loved us*,"—your hearts will be satisfied as with marrow and fatness. If the exceeding love of God in Christ Jesus shall be shed abroad in your hearts by the Holy Spirit, you will want no sermon from me:

your inward experience will be better than any discourse. May your love, like a drop of dew, be exhaled and carried up into the boundless heaven of God's love; may your heart ascend to the place where your treasure is, and rest itself upon the heart of God. Blessed shall you be if in your hearts Christ's love and yours shall both be fully known and felt at this moment. O, blessed Spirit, cause it to be so. Thus should we have the text in action, and that is a thousand times better than the mere quiet letter. If you have visited the picture galleries at Versailles, where you see the wars of France from the earliest ages set forth in glowing colours upon the canvas, you cannot but have been struck with the pictures, and interested in the terrible scenes. Upstairs in the same palace there is a vast collection of portraits. I have traversed those galleries of portraits without much interest, only here and there pausing to notice a remarkable countenance. Very few persons linger there, everybody seems to walk on as quickly as the polished floors allow. Now, why is it that you are interested by the portraits downstairs and not by those upstairs? They are the same people; very many of them in the same dress; why do you not gaze upon them with interest? The reason lies here : the portrait in still life, as a rule, can never have the attraction which surrounds a scene of stirring action. There you see the warrior dealing a terrible blow with his battle axe, or the senator delivering himself of an oration in the assembly, and you think more of them than of the same bodies and faces in repose. Life is impressive; action awakens thought. It is just so with the text. Look at it as a matter of doctrinal statement; "We love him, because he first loved us," and if you are a thoughtful person you will consider it well; but feel the fact itself, feel the love of God, know it within our own souls, and manifest it in our lives, and how engrossing it becomes. May it be so by the power of the Holy Spirit this morning; may you be loving God while you are hearing, and may I be loving him intensely while I am preaching.

With this as an introduction, I shall use the text for four purposes; first, *for doctrinal instruction;* then *for experimental information;* thirdly, *for practical direction;* and fourthly, *for argumentative defence.*

I. We shall use the text briefly for DOCTRINAL INSTRUCTION; and one point of doctrinal instruction is very clear, namely, that *God's love to his people is first.* "He first loved us." Now, make sure of this point of doctrine, because forgetfulness about it is connected with much error, and with more ignorance. The love of God to us precedes our love to God. According to Scripture it must be first in the most eminent sense. because it is eternal. The Lord chose his people in Christ Jesus from before the foundations of the world, and to each one of his people that text may be applied,—" Yea, I have loved thee with an everlasting love." His mercy is from everlasting to them that fear him. From all eternity the Lord looked upon his people with an eye of love, and as nothing can be before eternity, his love was *first.* Certainly he loved us before we had a being, for did he not give his Son to die for us nearly nineteen hundred years ago, long before our infant cries had saluted our mother's ear? He loved us before we had any desire to be loved by him, yea when we were provoking him to his face, and displaying the fierce enmity of our unrenewed hearts. Remember "his great love wherewith he loved us even when we were dead in sin." "God commendeth his love toward us, in that, while we were yet sinners, Christ died for us." When we had not as yet one throb of spiritual feeling; one pulse of hope, or one breathing of desire, the Lord loved us even then.

The love of God is before our seeking ; he draws us before we run after him. We do not seek that love ; that love seeks us. We wander further and further from it, resist it, and prove ourselves unworthy of it : such are our nature and our practice, that they offer nothing congenial to divine love, but the love of God arises in its freeness and stays our mad career by its power over the conscience and the will. "Ye have not chosen me, but I have chosen you," is the voice of sovereign grace ; let our response be, "By the grace of God we are what we are."

The Lord's love is before any repentance on our part. Impenitent sinners never would repent if God did not love them first. The Lord hates sin, but yet he loves sinners ; he compassionately loved us when sin was pleasant to us, when we rolled it under our tongue as a sweet morsel, when neither the thunders of his law nor the wooings of his gospel could persuade us to turn from it. When in our bosoms there were no convictions of sin, when there were no evangelical lamentations because of offences against a gracious God, he loved us then. To-day brethren we are possessors of faith in Jesus Christ, but our faith in Jesus Christ did not come before his love ; on the contrary, our faith rests in what that love has done for us of old. When we were unbelieving and hard of heart, and resisted the testimony of the Holy Spirit, and put from us the word of eternal life, even then the Lord pitied us, and had mercy upon us ; and continued still to invite, still to entreat, still to persuade, till at last the happy hour came when we believed and entered into a sense of his love. There are many things about you now, beloved of the Lord, which are the objects of divine approbation, but they were not there at first ; they did not precede divine love, but are the fruits of it. To use an old English word which has somewhat lost its meaning, the love of God is *preventing* love—it goes before any right motions of the soul, and in order of time it is *first*, before any desires, wishes, aspirations, or prayers on our part. Are you this day devout ? Yet he loved you not at the first because you were devout, for originally you were not so : his love was first before your devotion. Are you this day holy ? Blessed be his name for it ; but he loved you when you were unholy ; your holiness follows upon his love, he chose you that you might be holy. You are becoming like him by the sanctifying influences of his blessed Spirit, and he loves his image in you, but he loved you when that image was not there : yea he looked on you with infinite compassion when you were heirs of wrath even as others, and the image of the devil was conspicuous both upon your character and your nature. However early in life you began to love the Lord, his love was first. This is very wonderful, but blessed be his name, we know that it is true, and we rejoice in it.

The fact is that the love of God, as far as we know anything about it, had no reason derived from us upon which to ground itself. He loved us because he would love us, or, as our Lord put it, "Even so, Father ; for so it seemed good in thy sight." He had reasons in his own nature, good reasons, fetched from the best conceivable place, namely from his own perfections ; but those reasons he has not been pleased to communicate to us. He bids us know that he will have mercy on whom he will have mercy, and will have compassion on whom he will have compassion. Thus he tries the loyal submissiveness of our hearts, and I trust we are able to bow in reverent silence to his righteous will.

Divine love is its own cause, and does not derive its streams from anything in us whatsoever. It flows spontaneously from the heart of God, finding its deep wellsprings within his own bosom. This is a great comfort to us, because, being uncreated, it is unchangeable. If it had been set upon us because of some goodness in us, then when the goodness was diminished the love would diminish too. If God had loved us second and not first, or had the cause of the love been in us, that cause might have altered, and the supposed effect, namely, his love, would have altered too; but now, whatever may be the believer's condition to-day, however he may have wandered, and however much he may be groaning under a sense of sin, the Lord declares, " I do earnestly remember him still." The Lord did not love you at first because you had no sin; he foreknew all the sin you ever would have, it was all present before his sacred mind, and yet he loved you, and he loves you still. " I am God; I change not; therefore ye sons of Jacob are not consumed." O blessed love of God, since thou art first we will give thee the first place in our thoughts, the highest throne in our hearts, the royal position in our souls; glorifying thee, for thou art first !

Another part of the doctrine of the text is this, that *the love of God is the cause of our love to God.* A thing may be first and another second, and yet the first may not be the cause of the second, there may be no actual link between the two : but here we have it unmistakeably, " We love him *because* he first loved us"; which signifies not merely that this is the motive of which we are conscious in our love, but that this is the force, the divine power, which created love in us. I put it to you, should we have loved God had he not first given his Son to die for us ? Had there been no redeeming sacrifice should we have had any love to God ? Unredeemed men, left to go on like fallen angels in their sin, would have had no more love to God than fallen angels have. How could they ? But the Son given to redeem is the great foundation of love. God gives his Son, and so reveals his own love and creates ours. Is not his love seen to be the cause of ours when we remember Calvary ?

But he might have given his Son to die for men, beloved, and yet you and I might not have loved him, because we might not have been aware of the great fact. It is no small grace on God's part that "to you is the word of this salvation sent." While the heathen have never heard it, by the arrangement of his gracious providence you have been favoured with the good news. You have it in your homes in the form of the Holy Scriptures, you hear it every Sabbath day from the pulpit. How would you have ever come to love him if he had not sent his gospel to you ? The gift of his Son Jesus, and the providence which leads the herald of mercy to the saved one's door, are evident causes of man's love to God. But more than this, Christ died and the gospel is preached, and yet some men do not love him. Why not ? Because of the hardness of their hearts. But others do love him : shall I trace this to the natural betterness of their hearts ? I dare not, and much less do they. There is no believer who would ask me to do so in his own case; but I must trace it to the influence of the Holy Spirit, going with the revelation of the love of God in Christ Jesus, affecting the heart, and creating faith and love and every grace in the soul. Beloved, if you love God, it is with no love of yours, but with the love which he has planted in your bosoms. Unrenewed human nature is a soil in which love to God will not grow. There must be a taking away of the rock, and a supernatural change of the barren ground into good soil, and then, as a rare plant from another land, love must be planted in our hearts and sustained by power divine, or else it never will be found there. There is no love to God in this world that is of the right kind except that which was created and formed by the love of God in the soul.

Put the two truths together, that the love of God is first, and that the love of God is the cause of our love, and I think you will be inclined henceforth to be believers in what are commonly called the doctrines of grace. To me it is very wonderful that they are not received by all churches, because they are practically acknowledged by all Christians on their knees. They may preach as they like, but they all pray according to the doctrines of grace; and those doctrines are so consistent with the Christian's experience, that it is notable that the older a believer becomes, and the more deeply he searches into divine truth, the more inclined he is to give the whole of the praise of his salvation to the grace of God, and to believe in those precious truths which magnify, not the free will of man, but the free grace of the Ever Blessed. I want no better statement of my own doctrinal belief than this, " We love him, because he first loved us." I know it has been said that he loved us on the foresight of our faith and love and holiness. Of course the Lord had a clear foresight of all these, but remember that he had also the foresight of our want of love, and our want of faith, and our wanderings, and our sins, and surely his foresight in one direction must be supposed to operate as well as his foresight in the other direction. Recollect also that God himself did not foresee that there would be any love to him in us arising out of ourselves, for there never has been any, and there never will be ; he only foresaw that we should believe because he gave us faith, he foresaw that we should repent because his Spirit would work repentance in us, he foresaw that we should love, because he wrought that love within us ; and is there anything in the foresight that he means to give us such things that can account for his giving us such things ? The case is self-evident—his foresight of what he means to do cannot be his reason for doing it. His own eternal purpose has made the gracious difference between the saved and those who wilfully perish in sin. Let us give all the glory to his holy name, for to him all the glory belongs. His preventing grace must have all the honour.

II. Secondly, we shall use the text FOR EXPERIMENTAL INFORMA-TION ; and here, first, we learn that *all true believers love God.* "We love him," and we all love him for one reason, "because he first loved us." All the children of God love their Father. I do not say that they all feel an equal love, or that they all feel as much love as they should : who among us does ? I will not say that they do not sometimes give cause to doubt their love; nay, I will urge that it is well for them to examine themselves even as Christ examined Peter, and said, "Simon, son of Jonas, lovest thou me?" But there is love in the heart of every true-born child of God; it is as needful to spiritual life as blood is to natural life. Rest assured there has never been born into the kingdom of God one solitary individual destitute of love to God. You may be deficient in some virtues (you should not be), but yet the root of the matter may be in you; but if you be without love you are as a sounding brass and as a tinkling cymbal, and whatever your outer works, though you give your body to be burned, and all your goods to feed the poor, yet, if there be no love to God in your soul, the mark of God's sheep is not upon you, and your spot is not the spot of his children. Rest assured that whosoever is born of God loveth God.

Observe carefully *the kind of love which is essential to every Christian* —"We love him, because he first loved us." Much has been said about disinterested love to God; there may be such a thing, and it may be very admirable, but it is not mentioned here. I trust, beloved, we know what it is to love God because of his superlative excellence and goodness, and surely the more we know him the more we shall love him for what he is, but yet unless we love him because he first loved us, whatever other sort of love we may have or think we have, it does not prove us to be children of God. This is the love we must have; the other form of love, if it be true, will grow up in us afterwards; that however, is not essential, nor need we exalt it unduly: loving God because he first loved us is a sufficient evidence of grace in the soul. Gratitude has been vilified as a mean virtue, but indeed it is a noble emotion, and is one of the most forcible of spiritual motives. Let a man love God admiringly because of what he is, but yet there must run side by side with it this grateful love of God, because he first loved him, or else he lacks that which John says is to be found in all the saints. Beloved, do not vex yourselves about any supposed higher degrees, but see to it that you love him because he first loved you. You may not be able to rise into those heights into which others of your brethren have ascended because you are as yet only a babe in grace; but you are safe enough, if your love be of this simple character, that it loves because it is loved.

Within this humble form of love which is so essential, there dwells a gracious sense of unworthiness, so needful to a true Christian. We feel that we did not deserve the love which God sheds upon us, and this humility we must have, or we lack one mark of a child of God. There is also in this lowly form of gracious affection a clear recognition of the fact that the Lord's love is graciously bestowed, and this also is essential to a Christian, and becomes to him the main source of his obedience and affection. If a man only loves me as much as I deserve to be loved, I do not feel under any very strong obligations, and consequently do not feel any very intense gratitude, but because the Lord's love is all of pure grace and comes to us as utterly undeserving ones, therefore we love him in return. See whether such a humble, grateful love towards God dwells in your hearts, for it is a vital point.

Love to God wherever it is found is a sure evidence of the salvation of its possessor. If you love the Lord in the sense described, then he loved you first, and loves you now. You want no other evidence but this to assure yourself that you abide in the love of God—that you love him.

I was told by a venerable brother some little time ago a story of our famous preacher, Robert Hall. He charmed the most learned by the majesty of his eloquence, but he was as simple as he was great, and he was never happier than when conversing with poor believers upon experimental godliness. He was accustomed to make his journeys on horseback, and having been preaching at Clipstone he was on his way home, when he was stopped by a heavy fall of snow at the little village of Sibbertoft. The good man who kept the "Black Swan," a little village hostelry, came to his door and besought the preacher to take refuge beneath his roof, assuring him that it would give him great joy to welcome him. Mr. Hall knew him to be one of the most sincere Christians in the neighbourhood, and therefore got off his horse and went into the little inn. The good man was delighted to provide for him a bed, and a stool, and a candlestick in the prophet's chamber, for that rustic inn contained such an apartment. After Mr. Hall had rested awhile by the fire the landlord said. "You must needs stop here all night, sir; and if you do not mind I will call in a few of my neighbours, and if you feel that you could give us a sermon in my taproom they will all be glad to hear you." "So let it be, sir," said Mr. Hall, and so it was: the taproom became his cathedral, and the "Black Swan" the sign of the gospel banner. The peasants came together, and the man of God poured out his soul before them wondrously. They would never forget it, for to hear Mr. Hall was an event in any man's life. After all were gone Mr. Hall sat down, and there came over him a fit of depression: out of which he strove to rise by conversation with his host. "Ah, sir," said the great preacher, "I am much burdened, and am led to question my own condition before God. Tell me now what you think is a sure evidence that a man is a child of God." "Well, Mr. Hall," said the plain man, "I am sorry to see you so tried; you doubt yourself, but nobody else has any doubt about you. I hope the Lord will cheer and comfort you, but I am afraid I am not qualified to do it." "Never mind, friend, never mind, tell me what you think the best evidence of a child of God?" "Well, I should say, sir," said he, "*if a man loves God* he must be one of God's children." "Say you so," said the mighty preacher, "then it is well with me," and at that signal he began to magnify the Lord at such a rate that his hearer afterwards said that it was wonderful to hear him, as for about an hour he went on with glowing earnestness, declaring the loveliness of God. "O sir," said he who told the tale, "you should have heard him. He said, 'Love God, sir. Why I cannot help loving him, how could I do otherwise?' And then he went on to speak about the Almighty and his love and grace, extolling the Lord's greatness, and goodness, and glory in redemption, and all that he did for his people, till he said, 'Thank you, thank you, my friend, if love to him is an evidence of being God's child, I know I have it, for I cannot help loving him. I take no credit to myself; he is such a lovely being, and has done so much for us, that I should be more brutish than any man if I did not love and adore him.'" That which cheered that good and great man's heart may, perhaps, cheer yours. If you are loving God you must have been loved of God: true love could not have come into your heart in any other conceivable way; and you may rest assured that you are the object of his eternal choice.

But oh, *if you do not love God, dear hearer, I invite you to think for a minute upon your state!* Hear of God and not love him? You must be blind. Know anything about his character and not adore him? Your heart must be like the heart of Nabal when it was turned into a stone. See God in Christ bleeding on the cross for his enemies and not love him! O Hell, thou canst not be guilty of a worse offence than this! Herein is love, shall it have no acknowledgment? It is said that a man cannot feel that he is loved without in some measure returning the flame: but what shall I say of a mind which beholds Christ's love but feels no love in return? It is brutish, it is devilish. God have mercy upon it. Breathe you the same prayer, O unloving heart, and say, "Lord, forgive me, and by thy Holy Spirit renew me, and give me henceforth to be able to say, 'I also in my humble fashion love God because he first loved me.'"

III. Thirdly, we shall use the text as a matter OF PRACTICAL DIRECTION. I earnestly trust that there are some here who, although they do not love God at present, yet desire to do so. Well, dear friend, *the text tells you how to love God.* You say, perhaps, "Oh, I shall love God when I have improved my character, and when I have attended to the external duties of religion." But are you going to get love to God out of yourself? Is it there, then? "No," say you. How, then, will you get it from where it is not? You may go often to an empty iron safe before you will bring a thousand pound note out of it, and you may look a long time to your own heart before you will bring out of it a love to God which is not there. What is the way by which a heart may be made to love God? The text shows us the method of the Holy Spirit. He reveals the love of God to the heart, and then the heart loves God in return. If, then, you are aroused this morning to desire to love God, use the method which the text suggests,—meditate upon the great love of God to man, especially upon this, "God so loved the world that he gave his only begotten Son that whosoever believeth in him should not perish, but have everlasting life." See clearly that you have by faith to trust your soul with Christ, and perceive that it is vast love which sets before you such a way of salvation in which the only thing required of you is that you be nothing, and trust Christ to be everything, and even that faith he gives you as a gift of his Spirit, so that the plan of salvation is all of love. If you want to repent, do not so much consider your sin as the love of Jesus in suffering for your sin; if you desire to believe, do not so much study the doctrine as study the person of Jesus Christ upon the cross, and if you desire to love, think over perpetually, till it breaks your heart, the great love of Jesus Christ in laying down his life for his worthless foes. The love of God is the birthplace of holy love. Not there in your hearts where you are attempting an absurdly impossible feat, namely, to create love in the carnal mind which cannot be reconciled to God ; but there in the heart of Jesus must love be born, and then it shall come down to you. You cannot force your mind into the condition of believing even a common thing, nor can you sit there and say, " I will love so and so," of whom you know nothing. Faith and love are second steps arising out of former steps. " Faith cometh by hearing," and love comes by contemplation ; it flows out of a sense of the love of Christ in the soul even as wine flows from the clusters in the wine-press. Go thou to the fragrant mystery of redeeming love, and tarry with it till in those beds of spices thine own garments shall be made to smell of myrrh and aloes and cassia. There is no way of sweetening thyself but by tasting the sweetness of Jesus Christ ; the honey of his love will make thy whole nature to be as a honeycomb, every cell of thy manhood shall drop sweetness.

Brethren, if we wish to sustain the love we have received, we must do the same thing. At the present moment you are loving God, and desire still to love him ; be wise, then, and feed love on love, it is its best food. This is the honey which will keep your sweetness sweet ; this is the fire which will keep your flame flaming. Could we be separated from the love of Christ our love would die out like a lamp in yonder streets when cut off from the main. He who quickened us into the life of love must keep us alive, or we shall become loveless and lifeless.

And if, perchance, your love has grown somewhat cold; if you long to revive it, do not begin by doubting God's love to you ; that is not the way of reviving but of weakening love. Believe in divine love, my brother, over the head of the coldness of your heart ; trust in Jesus Christ as a sinner if you cannot rejoice in him as a saint, and you will get your love back again. You see the flowing fountain, how it gushes with a constant stream ; and here I bring a pitcher and set it down, so that the stream rushes into it and fills it till it overflows. In this manner our souls ought to be filled with the love of Christ. But you have taken away your pitcher, and it has become empty, and now you say to yourself, " Alas, alas, there is nothing here ! What shall I do ? This pitcher is empty." Do ? Why do what you did at first ; go and set it under the flowing stream, and it will soon be full again ; but it will never get full by your removing it into a dry place. Doubting is the death of love ; only by the hand of faith can love be fed with the bread of heaven. Your tears will not fill it ; you may groan into it, but sighs and moans will not fill it ; only the flowing fountain can fill the vacuum. Believe thou that God loves thee still : even if thou be not a saint, believe thou in the mighty love of Christ towards sinners, and trust thyself with him, and then his love will come pouring in till thy heart is full again to overflowing. If you want to rise to the very highest state of love to Christ, if you desire to enjoy delights ecstatic, or to be perfectly consecrated, if you aim at an apostle's self-denial, or at a martyr's heroism, or if you would be as like to Christ as the spirits are in heaven, no tool can grave you to this image but love, no force can fashion you to the model of Christ Jesus but the love of Jesus Christ shed abroad in your soul by the Holy Ghost. Keep to this, then, as a matter of practical direction. Dwell in the love of God to you that you may feel intense love to God.

Once more, as a practical direction, *if you love God show it as God showed his love to you.* You cannot do so in the same degree, but you may in the same manner. God loved the worthless; love ye the worthless. God loved his enemies; love ye your enemies. The Lord loved them practically: love not in word only, but in deed and in truth. He loved them to self-sacrifice, so that Jesus gave himself for us: love ye to self-sacrifice also. Love God so that you could die a thousand deaths for him: love him till you make no provision for the flesh, but live alone for his glory; let your heart burn with a flame that shall consume you till the zeal of God's house shall have eaten you up. "We love him, *because* he first loved us," therefore let us love him as he loved us; let his love be both motive and model to us.

> "Lov'd of my God, for him again,
>   With love intense I burn;
> Chosen of him ere time began,
>   I choose him in return."

IV. Our text suggests to us AN ARGUMENTATIVE DEFENCE. You will see what I mean when I observe first, that our love to God seems to want an apology. We have heard of an emperor casting eyes of love upon a peasant girl. It would have been monstrous for her to have first looked up to him as likely to be her husband; everybody would have thought her to be bereft of her senses had she done so; but when the monarch looked down upon her and asked her to be his queen, that was another thing. She might take leave to love from his love. Often does my soul say, "O God, I cannot help loving thee, but may I? Can this poor heart of mine be suffered to send up its love to thee? I, polluted and defiled, nothingness and emptiness and sinfulness, may I say, 'Yet do I love thee, O my God, almighty as thou art'? 'Holy, holy, holy,' is the salutation of the seraphim, but may I say 'I love thee, O my God'?" Yes, I may, because he first loved me. There is love's license to soar so high.

> "Yet I may love thee too, O Lord,
>   Almighty as thou art,
> For thou hast stoop'd to ask of me
>   The love of my poor heart."

Then, again, if any should enquire of us as they did of the sponse,

" What is thy beloved more than another beloved, O thou fairest among women ? what is thy beloved more than another beloved, that thou dost so charge us ? What is this passion that you have for God, this love you bear to his incarnate Son ?" we have a conclusive argument as against them, even as we had a quietus for our own fears. We reply, " We love him, because he first loved us, and if you did but know that he loved you, if you did but know that he has done for you what he has done for us, you would love him too. You would not want to ask us why, you would wonder why you do not love him too."

> " His love if all the nations knew,
> Sure the whole world will love him too."

We shall not want to all eternity any other defence for loving God than this, " Because he first loved us."

Here is also an argument for the lover of the old orthodox faith. It has been said by some that the doctrines of grace lead to licentiousness, but our text is a most excellent shield against that attack. Brethren, we believe that the Lord loved us, first, and most freely, not because of our tears or prayers, nor because of our foreseen faith, nor because of any-thing in us, but *first*. Well, what comes out of that ? Do we therefore say, " If he loved us when we were in sin, let us continue in sin that grace may abound," as some have wickedly said ? God forbid. The inference we draw is, " We love him, because he first loved us." Some can be swayed to morality by fear, but the Christian is sweetly drawn to holiness by love. We love him, not because we are afraid of being cast into hell if we do not—that fear is gone, we who are justified by God can never be condemned ; nor because we are afraid of missing heaven, for the inheritance is entailed upon as many of us as are joint heirs with Jesus Christ. Does this blessed security lead us to carelessness ? No, but in proportion as we see the greatness and the infinity of the love of God, we love him in return, and that love is the basis of all holiness, and the groundwork of a godly character. The doctrine of grace, though often maligned, has proved in the hearts of those who have believed it to be the grandest stimulus to heroic virtue, and he who affirms otherwise knows not what he says.

Last of all, here is a noble argument to silence a gainsaying world. Do you see what a wonderful text we have here ? It is a description of Christianity. Men say they are weary of the old faith, and beg us to advance with the times—how shall we reply to them ? They want something better, do they ? The philosophers who pander to the age are going to give it a better religion than Christianity ! Are they ? Let us see. We shall, however, wait very long before their false pro-mises will approximate to fulfilment. Let us rather look at what we we really have already. Our text is a circle. Here is love descending from heaven down to man, and here is love ascending from man to God, and so the circle is completed. The text treats alone of love. We love the Lord, and he loves us. The text resembles Anacreon's harp. which resounded love alone. Here is no word of strife, selfishness, anger, or envy ; all is love, and love alone. Now, it comes to pass that out of this love between God and his people there grows (see the context of my text) love to men, for " he that loveth God loveth his brother also." The ethical essence of Christianity is love, and the great master doctrine that we preach when we preach Jesus Christ is this— " God has loved us, we love God, and now we must love one another." O ye nations, what gospel do you desire better than this ? This it is that will put aside your drums, your cannons, and your swords. When men love God and love each other, what need for all the blood-stained pageantry of war ? And this will end your slavery, for who will call his brother his slave when he has learned to love the image of God in every man ? Who is he that will oppress and domineer when he has learned to love his God and love the creatures God has made ? Behold, Christianity is the Magna Charta of the universe. Here is the true " Liberty, Equality, and Fraternity," which men will seek for in vain in politics ; here is the sacred Communism which will injure no man's rights, but will respect every man's griefs, and succour every man's needs ; here is, indeed, the birth principle of the golden age of peace and joy, when the lion shall eat straw like the ox, and the weaned child shall play on the cockatrice's den. Spread it, then, and let it circulate throughout the whole earth—God's love first, our love to him next, and then the universal love which shuts not out a man of any colour, of any class, or of any name, but calls upon itself to love both God and man, because God is loved.

The Lord bless this meditation to you, by his Spirit, for Christ's sake. Amen.

5. Life's Need and Maintenance

"None can keep alive his own soul."—Psalm xxii. 29.

WE must commence by noticing the connection, that we may arrive at the first meaning of the words. There is a day coming when the true God will be acknowledged as Lord and God by all mankind, for the twenty-seventh verse tells us—"All the ends of the world shall remember and turn unto the Lord: and all the kindreds of the nations shall worship before thee." In that day the greatest of men will bow before him. The verse from which we cull our text says: "All they that be fat upon earth shall eat and worship." The prosperous ones, those who have grown rich and great, shall receive good at the hands of the Saviour, and shall rejoice to adore him as the author of their fatness. Kings shall own him as their King, and lords accept him as their Lord. Then shall not only the riches of life, but the poverty of death also, render him homage, for as men shall go down to the dust of the grave, in their feebleness and weakness they shall look up to him for strength and solace, and shall find it sweet to worship him in death. Men shall know that the keys of death are in his hands. "All they that go down to the dust shall bow before him," and it shall be known all the world over that the issues of life are in the hands of Jesus Christ; they shall understand that he is appointed as Mediator to rule over all mortal things, for the government shall be upon his shoulder; he shall open and no man shall shut, and shut and no man shall open, for it is his sovereign prerogative to kill and to make alive, and "none can keep alive his own soul." I pass on from this meaning with the hopeful belief that this dispensation is not to end, as some suppose, without the conquest of the world to Christ. Surely "all kings shall bow before him, all nations shall serve him." The shame of the cross shall be followed by honour and glory, "men shall be blessed in him, all nations shall call him blessed." The conviction grows with me every day, the more I read the Scriptures, that the disheartening views of some interpreters are not true, but that ere the whole of prophecy

45

shall be wrought out into history the kingdoms of this world shall become the kingdoms of our Lord and of his Christ.

Leaving this, we come to consider a more spiritual meaning, which we believe to be as truly the sense of the passage as the other. You will notice, if you read the psalm carefully, when you come to its close, that our Saviour seems to delight himself in being made food for the saved ones among the sons of men. In the 26th verse he says, " The meek shall eat and be satisfied." Here he is thinking of the poor among men, to whom he has ever been the source of abounding comfort : to them his gospel has been preached, and thousands of them have found in him food for their souls which has satisfied them, filled their mouths with praise, and made their hearts live for ever. The poor from the highways and hedges feast to the full at his royal table, yea, the blind, and the halt, and the lame, the very beggars of the streets are among his household guests. Christ is very mindful of the poor and needy, he redeems their soul from deceit and violence, and their blood is precious in his sight. Especially do the poor in spirit feed on Jesus ; over them he pronounced the first benediction of the sermon on the mount, and of them he declares " theirs is the kingdom of heaven." What a feast do poor perishing spirits enjoy in Jesus when his flesh becomes to them meat indeed, and his blood is drink indeed.

Nor is this all the feeding upon Christ, for in the 29th verse we hear of it again. Not only the poor feed upon the bread of heaven, but the great, the rich, and the strong live upon him too : " all they that be fat upon earth shall eat and worship," there is no other way of life for them, for " none can keep alive his own soul." The saints, too, when they have grown in grace, when they have supplied their hunger, and are fat and flourishing in the courts of the Lord's house, must still eat of the same heavenly food ; the fat need Jesus as much as the lean, the strong as much as the feeble, for none can do without him, " none can keep alive his own soul." Thus the rich and the poor meet together, and Jesus is the food of them all. The empty and the full alike draw near to the Redeemer's fulness and receive grace for grace.

Among those who feel their need of Jesus there are some of a mournful type of character, who count themselves ready to perish. They dare not number themselves among the meek who shall eat and be satisfied, much less could they think of themselves as the fat upon earth who shall eat and worship, but they stand back from the feast as utterly unworthy to draw near. They dare not believe themselves to be spiritually alive unto God, they reckon themselves among those that go down into the pit, they bear the sentence of death in themselves and are prisoners under bondage through fear. Their sense of sin and personal unworthiness is so conspicuous, and so painful, that they are afraid to claim the privileges of the living in Zion. They fear that their faith is expiring, their love is dying out, their hope is withered, and their joy clean departed. They compare themselves to the smoking flax, and think themselves to be even more offensive than the nauseous smell given forth by the smoking wick. To such comes the word which precedes my text— " They that go down to the dust shall bow before him." Christ shall be worshipped even by them ; their last moments shall be cheered by his presence. When through depression of spirit, through the assaults of Satan, and through inability to see the work of the Spirit in their souls, they shall be brought so low as to be down to the dust, they shall be lifted up from their misery and made to rejoice in the Lord their Redeemer, who will say unto them,—" Shake thyself from the dust ; arise and sit down : loose thyself from the bands of thy neck, O captive daughter of Zion." When souls are thus brought down they begin to learn for themselves that "none can keep alive his own soul." A poor broken-hearted spirit knows this, for he fears that the inner life within his soul is at its last gasp, and he is afraid that his faith and love, and all his graces will be as bones scattered at the grave's mouth, and then he learns what I trust we shall believe at this time without such a painful experience to teach it to us, namely, that none of us can keep our own soul alive, but that we must have food continually from above, and visitations of the Lord to preserve our spirits. Our life is not in ourselves, but in our Lord. Apart from him we could not exist spiritually, even for a moment. We cannot keep our own soul alive as to grace, That is to be the subject of this morning's meditation, and may the Holy Spirit render it profitable to us !

I. The first point of consideration out of which the rest will come is this—THE INNER LIFE MUST BE SUSTAINED BY GOD.

We are absolutely dependent upon God for the preservation of our spiritual life. We all of us know that none of us can *make* his own soul live. Thou hast destroyed thyself, but thou canst not make thyself to live again. Spiritual life must always be the gift of God ; it must come from without, it cannot arise from within. Between the ribs of death life never takes its birth ; how could it ? Shall the ocean beget fire, or darkness create light ? You shall go to the charnel house as long as you please, but, unless the trump of the resurrection shall sound there, the dry bones will remain in their corruption. The sinner is " dead in trespasses and sins," and he never will have even so much as a right desire towards God, nor a pulse of spiritual life, until Jesus Christ, who is " the resurrection and the life," shall quicken him. Now, it is important for us to remember that we are as much dependent upon the Lord Jesus and the power of his Spirit for being kept alive as we were for being made alive at the first. "None can keep alive his own soul." Do you remember when first you hung upon Christ for everything ? That same entire dependence must be exercised every day of your life, for there is need of it. You remember your former nakedness, your poverty, your emptiness, your misery, your death apart from Christ; remember that the case is not one whit better if you could now be separated from sin. If now you have any grace, or any holiness, or any love, you derive it entirely from him, and from moment to moment his grace must be continued to you ; for if connection between you and Christ should by any possibility be severed, you would cease spiritually to live. That is the truth we want to bring forward.

Here let us remark that this is not at all inconsistent with the undying nature of the spiritual life. When we were born again there was imparted to us a new and higher nature called the spirit. This is a fruit of the Spirit of God, and it can never die ; it is an " incorruptible seed which liveth and abideth for ever." When it is imparted to the soul it makes us partakers of the divine nature, and it keeps us so that the evil one toucheth us not so as utterly to destroy us. Yet this fact is quite consistent with the assertion that we cannot keep our own soul alive, for though we live it is because the Lord keeps us alive. The new-born nature is safe because the Lord protects it; it survives the deadly influences of the world because the Lord continues to quicken it. Our new nature is united to the person of Christ, and we live because he lives. We are not kept alive by independent power, but by perpetual renewal from the Lord.

This is true of every man living. "None can keep alive his own soul"—no, not one. You young people think, perhaps, that old Christians get on better than you do; you imagine that their experience preserves them, but indeed they cannot keep their own souls alive any more than you can. You tried and tempted ones sometimes look with envy upon those who dwell at ease, as though their spirituality was self-supporting, but no, they cannot keep their own souls alive any more than you can. You know your own difficulties, but you do not know those of others; rest assured, however, that to all men there are these difficulties, and that no man can keep his own soul alive.

This is the truth at all times: at no one moment can we keep ourselves alive. While sitting in this house of prayer you may dream that assuredly you can keep yourself here, but it is not so. You might sin the foulest of sins in your heart while sitting here, and you might grieve the Holy Spirit, and cloud your life for years while worshipping among the people of God. You are not able to keep your own soul alive in your happiest and holiest moments. From your knees you might rise to blaspheme, and from the communion table you might go to the seat of the scorner if you were left to yourself.

> " All our strength at once would fail us,
>   If deserted, Lord, by thee ;
> Nothing then could aught avail us,
>   Certain our defeat would be :
>   Those who hate us
> Thenceforth their desire would see."

I seldom find myself so much in danger as when I have been in close communion with God. After the most ecstatic devotion one is hardly prepared for the coarse temptations of this wicked world. When we come down, like Moses from the mount, if we encounter open sin, we are apt to grow indignant and break all the commandments in the vehemence of our wrath. The sudden change from the highest and holiest contemplations to the trifles and vexations of earth subjects the soul to so severe a trial that the poet did well to say—

> " We should suspect some danger nigh
> When we perceive too much delight."

Even when our delight is of a spiritual kind we are apt to be off our guard after having been filled with it, and then Satan avails himself of the opportunity. We are never safe unless the Lord keeps us. If we could take you, my brethren, place you in the society of saints, give you to keep perpetual Sabbath-day, make every meal a sacrament, and set you nothing to say or do but what should be directly calculated to promote the glory of God, yet even there you could not keep your

49

own soul alive. Adam in perfection could not keep himself in Paradise, how can his imperfect children be so proud as to rely upon their own steadfastness. Among angels there were those who kept not their first estate, how shall man then hope to stand except he be upheld.

Why is this? How know we that our text is true? We gather arguments from the analogies of nature. We do not find that we can keep our own bodies alive. We need divine preservation, or disease and death will soon make us their prey. We are not self-contained as to this mortal existence, any one of us, nay, not for five minutes can we live upon ourselves. Take away the atmospheric air and who could keep himself alive. The heaving lungs need their portion of air, and if they cannot be satisfied, the man soon becomes a corpse. Deprive us of food, leave us for a week without meat or drink, and see if we can keep our natural soul alive. Take away from us the means of warmth in the time when God's cold rules the year, and death would soon ensue. Now, if the physical life is not to be sustained by itself, much less can the higher and spiritual life; it must have food, it must have the Spirit to sustain it. The Scriptures present to us the figure of a member of the body which dies if severed from the vital organs, and of the branch which is dried up if cut off from the stem. Toplady versifies the thought and sings—

> "Quicken'd by thee, and kept alive,
> I flourish and bear fruit;
> My life I from thy sap derive,
> My vigour from thy root.
>
> "I can do nothing without thee;
> My strength is wholly thine:
> Wither'd and barren should I be,
> If sever'd from the vine."

Yonder lamp burns well, but its future shining is dependent upon a fresh supply of oil; the ship in rapid motion borrows force from the continuance of the wind, and the sails hang idle if the gale ceases; the river is full to the bank, but if the clouds should never again pour out their floods it would become a dry trackway. All things depend on others, and the whole upon the Great Supreme: nothing is self-sustained; save God himself no being necessarily exists, and even immortal souls are only so because he has set his seal upon them, and declared that they shall inherit life eternal, or in consequence of sin shall sink into everlasting punishment. Hence we are sure that "none can keep alive his own soul."

But we need not rely upon analogy, we can put the matter to the test. Could any believer among us keep any one of his graces alive? You, perhaps, are a sufferer, and hitherto you have been enabled to be patient: but suppose the Lord Jesus should withdraw his presence from you, and your pains should return again, ah, where will your patience be? Or, I will suppose you are a worker, and you have done great things for the Lord: like Samson you have been exceeding strong; but let the Lord be once withdrawn, and leave you to attempt his work alone, you will soon discover that you are as weak as other men, and will utterly fail. Holy joy, for instance, take that as a specimen: did you rejoice in the Lord this morning when you woke? It is very sweet to wake up and hear the birds singing within your heart, but you cannot maintain that joy, nay, not even for an hour, do what you will. "All my fresh springs are in thee," my God, and if I am to joy and rejoice thou must anoint me continually with the oil of gladness. Have you not sometimes thought in the morning, "I feel so peaceful and calm, so resigned to the divine will, I think I shall be able to keep up this placid spirit all day long." Perhaps you have done so, and if so I know you have praised God for it; but if you have become perturbed you have learned again that to will is present with you, but how to perform that which you would you find not. Well, if for any one fruit of the Spirit we are dependent upon the Lord, how much more will this be true as to the essential life from which each of these graces springs?

This truth is equally illustrated by our need of help in every *act* of the divine life. Dear friends, have you ever tried what it is to perform any spiritual act apart from the divine power? What a dull, dead affair it becomes! What a mechanical thing prayer is without the Spirit of God. It is a parrot's noise, and nothing more; a weariness, a slavish drudgery. How sweet it is to pray when the Spirit gives us feeling, unction, access with boldness, pleading power, faith, expectancy, and full fellowship; but if the Spirit of God be absent from us in prayer our infirmities prevail against us, and our supplication loses all prevalence. Did you ever resolve to praise God, and come into the congregation where the sweetest psalms were being sent to heaven, but could you praise God till the Holy Spirit came like a divine wind and loosed the fragrance of the flowers of your soul? You know you could not; you used the sacred words of the sweet singers of Israel, but hosannas languished on your tongue and your devotion died. I know that it is dreadful work to be bound to preach when one is not conscious of the aid of the Spirit of God! It is like pouring water out of bottomless buckets, or feeding hungry souls out of empty baskets. A true sermon such as God will bless no man can preach of himself; he might as well try to sound the archangel's trumpet. We must have thee, O blessed Spirit, or we fail! O God, we must have thy power, or every action that we perform is but the movement of an automaton, and not the acceptable act of a living, spiritual man.

Have you never, dear friends, had to know that you cannot keep alive your own soul by your own blunderings and failings, when you have resolved to be very wise and correct? Did you ever get into a self-sufficient state and say, "Now, I shall never fall into that temptation again, for I am the burnt child that dreads the fire," and yet into that very sin you have fallen. Have you not said, "Well, I understand that business; there is no need to wait upon God for direction in so simple a matter, for I am well up in every particular relating to it, and I can manage the affair very well?" And have you not acted as foolishly in the whole concern as the Israelites did in the affair of the Gibeonites, when they were deceived by the old shoes and clouted, and the mouldy bread, and asked no counsel of the Lord? I tell you our strength, whenever we have any, is our greatest weakness, and our fancied wisdom is our real folly. When we are weak we are strong. When in a sense of entire dependence upon God, we dare not trust ourselves, we are both wise and safe. Go, young man, even you who are a zealous Christian, go without your morning prayer into the house of business, and see what will befall you. Venture, my sister, down into your little family without having called upon God for guidance, and see what you will do. Go with a strong resolve that you will never be guilty of the weakness which dishonoured you a few days ago, and depend upon the strength of your own will, and the firmness of your own purpose, and see if you do not ere long discover to your shame how great your weakness is. Nay, try none of these experiments, but listen to the word which tells you "none can keep alive his own soul."

And now, should any think that he can keep his own soul alive, let me ask him to look at the enemies which surround him. A sheep in the midst of wolves is safe compared with the Christian in the midst of ungodly men. The world waylays us, the devil assaults us, behind every bush there lurks a foe. A spark in mid ocean is not more beset, a worm is not more defenceless. If the sight of foes without be not enough to make us confess our danger, look at the foes within. There is enough within thy soul, O Christian, though thou be one of the best of saints, to destroy thee in an hour unless the grace of God guard thee and keep thy passions in check, and prevent thy stubborn will from asserting its own rebellious determinations. Oh, what a powder magazine the human heart is, even at the best; if some of us have not been blown up it has been rather because Providence has kept away the sparks than because of there being any lack of powder within. Oh, may God keep us, for if he leaves us we want no devil to destroy us, we shall prove devils to ourselves; we shall need no tempters except the dire lusting after evil which now conceals itself so craftily within our own bosom.

Certainly, dear brethren, we may be quite sure that "none can keep alive his own soul" when we remember that in the gospel provision is made for keeping our soul alive. The Holy Spirit is given that he may continually quicken and preserve us, and Jesus Christ himself lives that we may live also. To what purpose would be all the splendid provisions and the special safeguards of the covenant of grace for the preservation of the spiritual life if that spiritual life could preserve itself? Why doth the Lord declare, "I the Lord do keep it," if it can keep itself? The granaries of Egypt, so full of corn, remind us that there is a famine in the land of Canaan: the treasures laid up in Christ Jesus assure us that we are in need of them. God's supplies are never superfluous, but are meant to meet real wants. Let us, then, all acknowledge that no man among us can keep alive his own soul.

II. This brings me, secondly and briefly, to notice that THIS TRUTH BRINGS GLORY TO CHRIST. "None can keep alive his own soul." Weakminded professors are prone to trust in man, but they have here an evident warning against such folly. How can they trust in a man who cannot keep alive his own soul? Shall I crouch at the feet of my fellow man and ask him to hear my confession and absolve me, when I know that he cannot keep alive his own soul? Shall I look up to him and call him "father in God," and expect to receive grace from the laying on of his hand, when I learn that he is a weak, sinful being like myself? He cannot keep alive his own soul, what can he do for me? If he lives before God he has to live upon the daily charity of the Most

High : what can he have to give to me ? Oh, look not to your fellow virgins for the oil of grace, for they have not enough for themselves and you ; and whatever name a man may dare to take, whether he be priest, father, or Pope, look not to him, but look to Jesus, in whom all fulness dwells.

The glory which redounds to Christ from our daily dependence is seen in his becoming to us our daily bread ; his flesh is meat indeed, and his blood is drink indeed, and we must feed upon these continually, or die. Eating is not an operation to be performed once only, but throughout life, and so we have to go to Jesus again and again and find sustenance in him as long as life lasts. Beloved, we honoured our Lord at first when he saved us, and through being daily dependent upon him we are led to honour him every day, and if we are right hearted we shall honour him more and more every day, as we more and more perceive our indebtedness to him. He is our daily bread whereon we feed continually, and the living water whereof we continually drink ; he is the light which everlastingly shines upon us, he is in fact daily to us our all in all ; and all this prevents our forgetting him. As at the first he saved us, so he saves us still ; and as at the first we prized him, we prize him still.

More than that, as our life is maintained, not only by him, but by our abiding in union with him, this leads us to abide in love towards him. Union is the source of communion and love. The wife remains a happy wife by loving fellowship with her husband. When the betrothed one is married to her beloved, the wedding day is not the end of it all ; the putting on of the ring is the beginning, not the end. And so, when we believe in Jesus, we are saved, but we must not idly feel " it is all done now." No, it is only begun. Now is the life of dependence, the life of faith, the life of obedience, the life of love, the life of union commenced, and it is to be continued for ever. This makes us love, honour, and adore our Lord Jesus, since we only live by being one with him.

We have also to remember that our life is daily supported by virtue of what the living Redeemer is still doing for us, as well as by receiving the fruit of his death, and of our spiritual union with him. He ever liveth to make intercession for us, and therefore he is " able to save to the uttermost them that come unto God by him." The life of the ascended Redeemer is intimately bound up with our life ;—" Because I live ye shall live also." How this honours Christ, for we are thus led to realize a living Saviour, and to love him as a living, breathing, acting person. It is a pity when men only think of a dead Saviour, or of a baby Saviour, carried in the Virgin's arms, as the church of Rome does ; it is our joy to have a living Christ, for while he lives we cannot die, and while he pleads we cannot be condemned. Thus we are led to remember him as a living Saviour, and to give him honour.

But oh, my brethren, what must be the fulness of Christ when all the grace which the saints have must come out of him, and not merely all they have had, but all they obtain every day comes from him. If there be any virtue, if there be any praise, if there be anything heavenly, if there be anything divine, of his fulness have we received it, and grace for grace. What must be that power which protects and preserves myriads

of saints from temptation, and keeps them amid perils as many as the
sands of the sea ! What must be that patience which watches over the
frail children of God in all their weaknesses and wanderings, in all their
sufferings, in all their infirmities ! What must be his grace which covers
all their sin, and what his strength which supports them under all their
trials ! What must the fountain head be, when the streams which flow
to any one of us are so deep that we cannot fathom them, so broad that
we cannot measure them ! Yet millions of happy spirits are each one
receiving as much as any one of us may be, and still there is a fulness
abiding in Christ the same as before, for it has pleased the Father that
in him should all fulness dwell. Not a saint lives a moment apart from
him, for "none can keep alive his own soul." The cries of babes in grace
and the shouts of strong men who divide the spoil, all come from the
life which he lends and the strength which he gives. Between the
gates of hell and the gates of heaven in all those pilgrims whose faces
are towards the royal city all the life is Christ's life, and all the strength
is Christ's strength, and he is in them, working in them to will and to
do of his own good pleasure. Blessed be the name of the Lord Jesus,
who thus supplies all his people. Does not this display the exceeding
riches of his grace ?

III. Thirdly and practically, THIS SUBJECT SUGGESTS THE PATH
OF WISDOM FOR OURSELVES. "None can keep alive his own soul,"
then, my dear brothers and sisters, what manner of persons ought we
to be ?

Let me have your earnest thoughts on this point for a minute. Do
not let any one among us look back to a certain day and say, "On that
occasion I was regenerated and converted, and that is enough." I fear
that some of you get into a very bad condition by saying, "If I can
prove that I was converted on such a day that will do." This is altogether unjustifiable talk. Conversion is a turning into the right road;
the next thing is to walk in it. The daily going on in that road is as
essential as the first starting if you would reach the desired end. To
strike the first blow is not all the battle; to him that overcometh the
crown is promised. To start in the race is nothing, many have done that
who have failed; but to hold out till you reach the winning post is the
great point of the matter. Perseverance is as necessary to a man's
salvation as conversion. Do remember this, you not only want grace to
begin with, but grace with which to abide in Christ Jesus.

Learn, also, that we should diligently use all those means whereby the
Lord communicates fresh support to our life. A man does not say,
"Well, I was born on such and such a day, that is enough for me." No,
the good man needs his daily meals to maintain him in existence. Being
alive, his next consideration is to keep alive, and therefore he does not
neglect eating, nor any operation which is essential to life. So you, dear
friends, must labour for the meat which endureth to life eternal, you must
feed on the bread of heaven. Study the Scriptures daily—I hope you do
not neglect that. Be much in private prayer, your life cannot be healthy
if the mercy seat be neglected. Do not forsake the assembling of yourselves together, as the manner of some is. Be eager to hear the word,
and endeavour both to understand and practise it. Gather with God's
people in their more spiritual meetings, when they join in prayer and

praise, for these are healthful means of sustaining the inner life. If you neglect these you cannot expect that grace will be strong within you, you may even question if there be any life at all. Still, remember that even if a man should eat and drink that would not keep him alive without the power of God, and many die with whom there is no lack either of air or food. You must, therefore, look beyond the outward means, to God himself to preserve your soul, and be it your daily prayer, "Oh Saviour, by whom I began to live, daily enable me to look to thee that I may draw continuous life from thy wounds, and live because thou livest." Take these things home and practise them.

Keep, dear friends, also clear of everything which has a tendency to destroy life. A sane man does not willingly take poison ; if he knew it he would not touch the cup in which it had been contained. We are careful to avoid any adulteration in our food which might be injurious to life and health : we have our chemists busily at work to analyse liquids, lest haply inadvertently we should imbibe death in the water which we drink. Brethren, now let us be equally careful as to our souls. Keep your chemist at work analysing the things of this life. Let conscience and understanding fit up their laboratory and prove all things. Analyse the sermon of the eloquent preacher, lest you drink in novelties of doctrine and arrant falsehoods, because he happens to put them prettily before you. Analyse each book you read, lest you should become tainted with error, while you are interested with the style and manner, smartness and elegance of your author. Analyse the company you keep ; test and try everything, lest haply you should be committing spiritual suicide, or carelessly squandering life away. Ask the Lord, the preserver of men, above all things, to keep you beneath the shadow of his wings, that you may not be afraid for the pestilence that walketh in darkness, nor for the destruction which wasteth at noonday, because his truth has become your shield and buckler, and you are safe.

Watch your life carefully, but look to Jesus Christ from day to day for everything. Do not become self-satisfied, so as to say, "Now I am rich and increased in goods." If ever a child of God imitates the rich man in the parable, and says, "Soul, take thine ease, thou hast much goods laid up for many years," he is a fool as much as the rich man was. I have known some become very exalted in spiritual things, the conflict is almost over with them, temptation has no power, they are masters of the situation, and their condition is of the most elevated kind. Well, ballooning is very pleasant to those who like it, but I think he is safest who keeps on the ground : I fear that spiritual ballooning has been very mischievous to a great many, and has turned their heads altogether. Their high conceit is falsehood. After all, my friend, to tell you the truth very plainly, you are no better than other people, though you think you are, and in one point I am sure you miserably fail, and that is in humility. When we hear you declare what a fine fellow you are, we suspect that you wear borrowed plumes, and are not what you seem. A peacock is a beautiful bird, what can be more brilliant ? But I am not enraptured with his voice, nor are you ; and so there may be fine feathers about certain people, perhaps a little too fine, but while they are showing themselves off, we know that there is a weak point about them, and we pray that it may not cause dishonour to the cause of

Christ. It is not our part to be hunting about for the failings of our fellow Christians, yet boasting has a tendency to make us examine the boaster. The practical thing is to believe that when we are proud ourselves there is something wrong about us. Whenever we stand before the looking-glass and think what fine fellows we are, we had better go at once to the great Physician and beseech him to give us medicine for our vanity. Mr. Peacock, you are certainly very handsome, but you should hear yourself croak. Professor, there are fine points about you, but there are sorry ones too : be humble and so be wise. Brother, if you get an inch above the ground you are just that inch too high. If you have anything apart from Christ, if you can live five minutes on past experience, if you think that you can live on yesterday's grace you make a mistake. You put the manna by so very cannily, you stored it up in the cupboard with such self-content. Go to it to-morrow morning instead of joining the rest of your brethren in gathering the fresh manna which will fall all around the camp. Go to the cupboard where you stored up yesterday's manna ! Ah, as soon as you open the door you close it again. Why did you shut that door so speedily ? Well, we need not look inside the cupboard, the smell is enough ; it has happened as Moses foretold it ; it has bred worms and it stinks as he said it would. Cover it up as quickly as you can. Dig a deep hole and throw it all in and bury it, that is the only thing to do with such rottenness. Day by day go to Christ and you will get your manna sweet, but begin to live on past or present attainments and they will breed worms and stink as sure as you are a man. Do not try it, for " none can keep alive his own soul."

IV. Last of all, THIS SUBJECT INDICATES A WAY OF USEFULNESS for every one here present who is a child of God. I think the great business of the Christian's life is to serve God, and that he can do mainly by aiming at the conversion of sinners. It is a grand thing to be blessed of God to turn sinners from the error of their ways; but listen, brethren, there is equally good work to be done by helping struggling saints. The old Roman said he thought it as much an honour to preserve a Roman citizen as to slay an enemy of his country, and he was right. There is as much acceptance before God in the work of instrumentally preserving souls alive as in being made the means of making souls to live at the first; the upholding of believers is as needful an exercise for Christian workers as the ingathering of unbelievers. I want you to think of this. If there is a person nearly drowned, a man will leap into the water to bring him out, and he gets great credit for it, and deserves it ; and so when a man saves a soul from death by earnest ministry, let him be glad and thank God. But if a man be starving, and ready to die, and you give him bread ; or if he be not reduced to that point, but would have been so had you not interfered, you have done as good an action in preserving life as the other friend who snatched life from between the jaws of death. You must never think little of the work which instructs the ignorant Christian, which clears the stumbling-blocks out of the way of the perplexed believer, which comforts the feeble-minded and supports the weak. These needful works must be done, while soul-saving must not be left undone. Perhaps some of you never will be the means of the conversion of many; then try to be the means of comfort to as many as you can. To be the means in the hand of the Holy Ghost of nurturing the life which God has given is a worthy service, and very acceptable with God. I would urge the members of this church to watch over one another. Be pastors to each other. Be very careful over the many young people that are come among us, and, if you see any backslide, in a gentle and affectionate manner endeavour to bring them back. Do you know any despondent ones? Lay yourselves out to comfort them. Do you see faults in any? Do not tell them of them hastily, but labour as God shall help you to teach them a better way. As the Lord often preserves you by the help of others, so in return seek to be in God's hands the means by which he shall keep your brethren from going astray, from sinking in despair, or from falling into error. I hold it out to you as a good and blessed work to do—will you try to accomplish it?

Now, if you say "Yes," and I think every Christian here says "Yes," then I am going to speak to you "concerning the collection, brethren." This is Hospital Sunday, and we must contribute our full share. Do you see any connection between this subject and the collection? I think I do. Here are these poor sick folk who will die unless they be carefully looked to, unless medicine and a physician's skill be provided for them. I know you are ready enough to look after sick souls; the point to which I have brought you is one which involves such readiness. Well, now, he who would look after a sick soul will be sure to care for a sick body. I hope you are not of the same class as the priest in the fable who was entreated by a beggar to give him a crown. "By no means," said the reverend father, "why should I give you a crown?" "Will you give me a shilling, holy father?" No, he would not give him a shilling, nor even a penny. "Then," said he, "holy father, will you of your charity give me a farthing?" No, he would not do anything of the sort. At last the beggar said, "Would not your reverence be kind enough to give me your blessing?" "Oh yes, my son, you shall have it at once; kneel down and receive it." But the man did not kneel down to receive it, for he reasoned that if it had been worth a farthing the holy father would not have given it to him, and so he went his way. Men have enough practical sense always to judge that if professed Christians do not care for their bodily wants, there cannot be much sincerity in their zeal for men's souls. If a man will give me spiritual bread in the form of a tract, but would not give me a piece of bread for my body, how can I think much of him? Let practical help to the poor go with the spiritual help which you render to them. If you would help to keep a brother's soul alive in the higher sense, be not backward to do it in the more ordinary way. You have an opportunity of proving your sincerity, and gratifying your charity, for the boxes will go round at once.

6. Marvellous Lovingkindness

"Shew thy marvellous lovingkindness."—Psalm xvii. 7.

THE Lord's people, in the time of their trouble, know where to go for comfort and relief. Being taught of God, they do not hew out to themselves broken cisterns, which can hold no water; but they turn to the ever-flowing fountain, they go to the well-head,—even to God himself; and there they cast themselves down, and drink to the full. David, when he wrote this Psalm, was evidently in very great distress; and, therefore, he says, "I have called upon thee, for thou wilt hear me, O God: incline thine ear unto me, and hear my speech." What he wanted was his God; as Dr. Watts expresses it,—

"In darkest shades if he appear,
  My dawning is begun;
He is my soul's sweet morning star,
  And he my rising sun."

Believers draw comfort both from God's ordinary and extra-ordinary dealings with them, for they regard God's lovingkindness as being both an ordinary and an extraordinary thing. I have heard of a good sister who, when a friend narrated to her some very gracious dealing of God, was asked the question, "Is it not very wonderful?" and she replied, "No; it is not wonderful, for it is just like him." Begging her pardon, and admitting the great truth that she meant to convey, I think it is still more wonderful that it should be "just like him." The wonder of extraordinary love is that God should make it such an ordinary thing, that he should give to us "marvellous lovingkindness," and yet should give it so often that it becomes a daily blessing, and yet remains marvellous still. The marvels of men, after you have seen them a few times, cease to excite any wonder. I suppose there is scarcely a building, however costly its materials, and however rare its architecture, as to which, sooner or later, you will not feel that you have seen enough of it. But God's wonderful works never pall upon you. You could gaze upon Mont Blanc, or you could stand and watch Niagara, yet never feel that you had exhausted all its marvels. And every-one knows how the ocean is never twice alike. They who live close to it, and look upon it every hour of the day, still see God's wonders in the deep.

That God should bless us every day, is a theme for our comfort. God's ordinary ways charm us. The verse before our text says, " ' I have called upon thee, for thou wilt hear me, O God.' I know thou wilt, for the blessing that I am about to ask from thee is a thing that I have been accustomed to receive from thee. I know thou wilt hear me, for thou hast heard me in the past; it is a habit of thine to listen to my supplications, and to grant my re-quests." I hope we can argue in a similar fashion; yet, at the same time, God's people draw equal comfort from the extraordinary character of the mercies he bestows upon them. They appeal to him to show them his " marvellous lovingkindness," to let them see the wonderful side of it as well as the common side of it, to let them behold his miracles of mercy, his extravagances of love, his superfluities of kindness;—I scarcely know what words to use when talking of what the apostle Paul calls "the riches of his grace, wherein he hath abounded toward us in all wisdom and prudence," " the exceeding riches of his grace in his kindness toward us through Christ Jesus."

I want, on this occasion, to dwell upon the extraordinary side of God's lovingkindness; and, using our text as a prayer, to say to the Lord in the language of David, "Shew thy marvellous loving-kindness." Sometimes, a man is brought into such a condition that he feels that, if God does not do something quite out of the common order of things, he will assuredly perish. He has now come to such a pass that, if some extraordinary grace is not displayed towards him, all is over with him. Well, now, such a brother may think that God will not give this extraordinary grace to him; he may be troubled at the idea that some marvellous thing is needed. It is to meet that suggestion of unbelief that I am going to address you now.

I. And my first remark is, that ALL THE LOVINGKINDNESS OF GOD IS MARVELLOUS.

The least mercy from God is a miracle. That God does not crush our sinful race, is a surprising mercy. That you and I should have been spared to live,—even though it were only to exist in direst poverty, or in sorest sickness,—that we should have been spared at all, after what we have been, and after what we have done, is a very marvellous thing. The explanation of the marvel is given in the Book of Malachi: "I am the Lord, I change not; therefore ye sons of Jacob are not consumed." If God had possessed such a short temper as men often have, he would have made short work with us all; but he is gracious and longsuffering, and there-fore he is very patient with us. The very least mercy that we ever receive from God is a very wonderful thing; but when we think of all that is meant by this blessed word "lovingkindness"—, which is a compound of all sorts of sweetnesses, a mixture of fragrances to make up one absolutely perfect perfume,—when we take that word "lovingkindness", and think over its meaning, we shall see that it is a marvellous thing indeed that it describes.

For, first, it is *marvellous for its antiquity*. To think that God should have had lovingkindness towards men or ever the earth was, that there should have been a covenant of election,—a plan of redemption,—a scheme of atonement,—that there should have been eternal thoughts of love in the mind of God towards such a strange being as man, is indeed marvellous. "What is man, that thou art mindful of him? and the son of man, that thou visitest him?" Read these words now with the tears in your eyes: "I have loved thee with an everlasting love: therefore with loving-kindness have I drawn thee;" and when you know that this passage refers to you, tell me if it is not "marvellous lovingkindness." God's mind is occupied with thoughts concerning things that are infinitely greater than the destiny of any one of us, or of all of us put together; yet he was pleased to think of us in love from all eternity, and to write our names upon his hands and upon his heart, and to keep the remembrance of us perpetually before him, for his "delights were with the sons of men." This antiquity makes it to be indeed "marvellous lovingkindness."

Next, think of *its discriminating character*, that God's loving-kindness should have come to the poorest, to the most illiterate, the most obscure, and often to the most guilty of our race. Remember what Paul wrote about this matter: "not many wise men after the flesh, not many mighty, not many noble, are called: but God hath chosen the foolish things of the world to confound the wise; and God hath chosen the weak things of the world to confound the things which are mighty; and base things of the world, and things which are despised, hath God chosen, yea, and things which are not, to bring to nought things that are: that no flesh should glory in his presence." Dr. Watts expresses the same thought in his verses,—

> "When the Eternal bows the skies
> To visit earthly things,
> With scorn divine he turns his eyes
> From towers of haughty kings.

> "He bids his awful chariot roll
> Far downward from the skies,
> To visit every humble soul,
> With pleasure in his eyes."

God's choice is marvellous. I know of no better word to apply to his lovingkindness to his chosen than that which is applied in the text: "thy marvellous lovingkindness."

> "What was there in you that could merit esteem,
>   Or give the Creator delight?
> 'Twas even so, Father,' you ever must sing,
>   'Because it seem'd good in thy sight.'"

There is no other explanation of this wondrous mercy, this " marvellous lovingkindness," than the poet gives,—

" His love, from eternity fix'd upon you,
Broke forth, and discover'd its flame,
When each with the cords of his kindness he drew,
And brought you to love his great name."

So, beloved, think over the antiquity of God's lovingkindness, and then of the discriminating character of it, and surely you will be full of adoring wonder.

After that, think also of *the self-sacrificing nature of his lovingkindness*,—that, when God had set his heart on man, and had chosen his people before the foundation of the world, then he should give—what? Himself. Ay, nothing short of that;—that he should not only give us this world, and his providence, and all its blessings, and the world to come, and all its glories; but that, in order to our possession of these things, he should give his own Son to die for us. Well might the apostle John write, " Herein is love, not that we loved God, but that he loved us, and sent his Son to be the propitiation for our sins." It was not that Christ died for us when we were righteous, " for scarcely for a righteous man will one die:" " but God commendeth his love toward us, in that, while we were yet sinners, Christ died for us." " When we were yet without strength, in due time Christ died for the ungodly." Isaiah had long before explained the mystery: " It pleased the Lord to bruise him: he hath put him to grief." You who love your children, to lose one of whom would be worse than to die, can realize a little of what must have been the Father's love to you in giving up his only-begotten Son that you might live through him. Dwell on this great truth, dear friends, meditate on it, and ask the Holy Spirit to lead you into its heights, and depths, and lengths, and breadths, for these lips cannot fully speak of its wonders. As you think over the Lord's ancient lovingkindnesses which were ever of old, his distinguishing love towards his redeemed, and his self-sacrificing love in giving up his Only-begotten, you will be obliged to say, " It is marvellous lovingkindness; it is marvellous lovingkindness indeed."

Then go on to think of *the marvellous constancy of it*. That one should begin to love another, is not so very wonderful; but that love, after it has been despised and ill-requited, should still continue,—that the sweet love of Christ should not long ago have curdled into jealousy, and from jealousy have soured into indignation, is an extraordinary thing. He loved us, brothers and sisters, when we did not even know him, and yet hated the Unknown; when we did not even dimly understand his love to us, and peradventure even ridiculed it, or at least neglected it. Yet he kept on loving us until he loved us into loving him. But even since then, what has been our character? Are you satisfied with what you have been towards the Well-beloved? Are you content with your conduct towards the Bridegroom of your souls? I trow that you are not; and yet, notwithstanding your lukewarmness, your backsliding, your dishonouring of his name, your unbelief, your pride, your love of others, he still loves you; and even now, if you are not enjoying fellowship with him, he has not gone away from you, for his word still is, "Behold, I stand at the door, and knock." He loves, he loves on, and he loves still. Many waters cannot quench his love, neither can the floods drown it. It is indeed "marvellous lovingkindness." Can you think of a better adjective than that? I cannot, yet I am conscious that even it does not fully express the miraculous character of this all-enduring love which will not take our "No" for an answer, but still says, "Yes,—'yea, I will betroth thee unto me in righteousness, and in judgment, and in lovingkindness, and in mercies. I will even betroth thee unto me in faithfulness: and thou shalt know the Lord.'" Oh, this wonderful, this matchless, this unparalleled, this inconceivable, this infinite love! No human language can adequately describe it, so let us sit still, and marvel at that which we cannot even understand.

There is much in God's lovingkindness to be marvelled at *in its strange ingenuity*. I might keep on with this topic for ever, applying one word and another to it; yet I should never have shown you even the tithe of its wonders, for it is an altogether inexhaustible theme. But it is wonderful how God deals with us with such a sacred ingenuity of tenderness. He seems to be always thinking of something for our good; while we, on our part, appear to be always testing his love in one way or another. Some fresh want is discovered only to receive a new supply of grace. Some fresh sin breaks out only to be blotted out with the ever-pardoning blood of Jesus. We get into fresh difficulties only to receive fresh aid. The further I go on my way to heaven, the more I do admire the road as well as wonder at the goal to which that road shall bring me. "O world of wonders!" said John Bunyan; "I can say no less." They tell us, nowadays, that the world is worn-out, and that there is no joy in life, and nothing fresh to afford delight. Ah, me! they talk of the attractions of fiction and of the playwright's art, and I know not what besides. They must needs travel all round the world to get a new sensation; and many a man, to-day, is like the Emperor Tiberius, who offered large sums of money to anyone who could invent a new pleasure, meaning, alas! too often, a new vice, or a new way of practising it. But staying at home with Christ has more wonders in it than gadding abroad with all the wisest of the world. There is more to marvel at in half an inch of the way to heaven than there is in a thousand leagues of the ordinary pathway of unbelieving men. They call their joys by the name of "life", and say that they must "see life"; but the apostle John tells us that "he that hath the Son hath life; and he that hath not the Son of God hath not life;" that is to say, he is dead. Death has its varieties of worms and rottenness; there are charnel-houses *and* charnel-houses, various processes and methods of corruption, and no doubt there is a science that men may learn in the cemetery, and call it life, if they like; but, oh! if they did but once see Christ upon the cross, they would learn that they had been blind till then. If they did but know his lovingkindness, they would rejoice in it in the sick-chamber, in the long weary night watches, when every bone prevented sleep; they would even recognize it in the arrows of death that smote wife, and child, and brother. They would see it, not only in the table loaded for the supply of hunger, and in the garments furnished against the cold, and in every common blessing of providence; but they would also see it in every despondency, in every deficiency, in every cross, and every loss; and, seeing it, they would keep on saying, " It is all for the best; it is all better than the best could have been if it had been left to me. It is marvellous; it is marvellous lovingkindness." I do believe that, when we get to heaven, one of the wonders of the glory-land will be to look back upon the road over which we have travelled. It will be marvellous to note the way in which God has led us; and we shall, as our hymn puts it,—

> " Sing with rapture and surprise,
> His lovingkindness in the skies."

I must now leave this part of my subject with you, only again urging you to think over the truth of which I have been speaking, that all God's lovingkindness to his people is marvellous.

II. Now, secondly, THIS LOVINGKINDNESS WE SHOULD DESIRE TO SEE. The psalmist says, " Shew thy marvellous lovingkindness;" and we ought to ask God to let us see it; and that, I think, in four ways.

First, *let me see it with my intellect, that I may adore.* Help me, O blessed Spirit, to see and understand what is the lovingkindness of God to my soul! I know that it is written of some that " they shall understand the lovingkindness of the Lord." Let me be among the number of those truly wise ones. O Lord, make me wise to see the end and design of thy providence as well as the providence itself! Make me wise to perceive how thou hast prepared thy grace to meet my depravity, how thou dost adapt thine upholdings to the slipperiness of the way, and to the feebleness of my feet. Often shed a ray of light upon some passage in my life which, otherwise, I could not comprehend; and let the light stay there till I begin to see and to know why thou didst this and why thou didst that. " Shew thy marvellous lovingkindness." I am sure, dear friends, that the lessons of a man's own life are too often neglected; but there is, in the life of any ordinary child of God,— let me pick you out wherever you may be, John, Mary, Thomas,— enough to fill you with wonder and admiration of the lovingkindness of the Lord if your mind be but sufficiently illuminated to perceive the hand of God in it, and to see what God purposed by it. He sometimes uses strange means for producing blessed results. With his sharp axe, he will cut down all our choice trees; as by a whirlwind or a tornado, he will devastate our gardens, and make our fields a desolation; and he will do it all in order that he may drive us away from the City of Destruction, and make us go on pilgrimage to the Celestial City, where the axe can never come, and the leaves will never fade. In his mysterious dealings with us, the Lord often seems to push us backward that we may go forward, and to deluge us with sorrow that he may immerse us into blessing. That is his way of working wondrously; and if we did but understand it, according to the prayer of the text, "Shew thy marvellous lovingkindness," we should be full of adoring wonder.

The next meaning I would give to this prayer would be, *Lord, show thy lovingkindness to my heart, that I may give thee thanks.* Lord, I know that thou hast been very good to me; but I pray thee to show my heart how good thou hast been, by letting me see how unworthy I have been of this thy kindness. It is very profitable, sometimes, to sit down, and rehearse the lovingkindness of God, mingling with it penitential reflections upon your own shortcoming. If you do this, you will at last break out with some such cry as this, "Why is all this mercy shown to me?" I know a dear brother in Christ, a clergyman, whose name is Curme; he divides it into two syllables, "*Cur me*," so as to make it mean, "Why me? Why is all this goodness given to me, Lord?" And that is a question which I, too, would fain ask, "Why me, Lord?"

> "Why was I made to hear thy voice,
>   And enter while there's room ;
> When thousands make a wretched choice,
>   And rather starve than come ?"

Is this kindness, and this, and this, all meant for me? Can it really be intended for me? Such reflections as these will make me realize more than ever how "marvellous" is God's "lovingkindness" to me, and will fill my soul with adoring gratitude and thanksgiving.

Then, next, we ought to pray the Lord to *show his "marvellous lovingkindness" to our faith, that we may again confide in him.* If he will cause the eye of our faith to see that he has this "marvellous lovingkindness" toward us, we shall be the more ready to rely upon him in all the straits into which we may yet be brought. Dost thou believe it, my dear friend? Brother in Christ, dost thou believe that God loves thee? Thou knowest how sweet it is to be sure that thy child loves thee. Though it may well do so, because of its many obligations to thee, yet is it sweet for its warm cheek to touch thine, and to hear it say, "Father, I love you." But, oh! it is sweeter far for God to say, "I love you." Read the Song of Solomon through, and be not afraid to appropriate the message of that sweet and matchless Canticle. Hear in it the voice of Jesus saying to thee, "Thou art all fair, my love; there is no spot in thee." "Thou hast ravished my heart, my sister, my spouse; thou hast ravished my heart with one of thine eyes, with one chain of thy neck." Such words as those may be sensuous to those who are sensuous, but they are deeply spiritual to those who are spiritual; and, oh, the bliss of having such words as those to come from the Christ of God to us! Why, sometimes, when our Lord thus speaks to us, we hardly know how to bear our excess of joy. I would not ask for a better holiday than to have one hour alone with Jesus; to be undisturbed by any earthly care, and just to think of nothing else but the love of God,—the love of God to me. Oh, that it now were shed abroad, in all its fulness, in this poor heart of mine! O love divine, what is there that can ever match thine inexpressible sweetness? Truly it is "marvellous lovingkindness." Again I ask you,—Do you believe this? Are you sure you do? Pray God to show it to your faith distinctly and clearly, so that you shall be absolutely sure of it, and practically depend upon it whenever you need it.

One other meaning of the text may be, *show thy "marvellous lovingkindness" to me now in my experience, that I may rest in thee.* Let me now, at this present moment, O my God, experience something of that lovingkindness in my soul, in whatever condition I may happen to be, that I may be so flooded with the consciousness of it that I may do nothing else but sit in solemn silence before thee, and adore thee, while beholding the blazing splendour of thy love! I cannot say any more about this part of my theme, but must leave you to fill up the gaps in the sermon. This is not a topic upon which one should venture to speak if he wants to say all that should or could be said upon it.

III. So, thirdly, dear friends, I remark that IT SHOULD BE OUR DESIRE—and there are times when it should especially be our desire —TO SEE THIS "MARVELLOUS LOVINGKINDNESS" OF GOD DISPLAYED TO US IN ITS MARVELLOUSNESS.

I will make plain to you what I mean directly; and, first, we would see it *as pardoning great sin.* I expect we have here, in this assembly, at least one whose sin lies very heavy on his conscience. We do not find many such people come out to week-evening services, but yet I thank God that they do come here. Your sin is very great, dear friend. I cannot exaggerate it, because your own sense of its greatness far surpasses any descriptions I could give. You feel that, if God were to pardon you, it would be a marvellous thing. If he were, in one moment, to take all your guilt away, and to send you home completely forgiven, it would be a marvellous thing. Yes, it would, it would; but I beg you to pray this prayer, "Lord, show forth thy marvellous lovingkindness in me." God is constantly doing wonders; then, glorify his name by believing that he can work this miracle of mercy for you. Do not be afraid even to sing,—

> "Great God of wonders! all thy ways
> Are matchless, God-like, and divine;
> But the fair glories of thy grace
> More God-like and unrivall'd shine:
> Who is a pardoning God like thee?
> Or who has grace so rich and free?"

Believe on the Lord Jesus Christ, and thou shalt be saved, and saved immediately. Trust him now; and marvellous though it will be to you, I have shown you that God's lovingkindness is all marvellous, and that the extraordinary is ordinary with God, and that the marvellous is but an every-day thing with him. Pray for this "marvellous lovingkindness" to be manifested to you, and you shall have it. One said, "If God ever saves me, he shall never hear the last of it." You may say the same, and resolve that, henceforth, having had much forgiven, you will love much; having been saved from great sin, you will tell it on earth, and tell it in heaven; and, if you could, you would even wish to make hell itself resound with the wondrous story,—

> " 'Tell it unto sinners tell,
> I am, I am out of hell;'—

"and what is more, I am on the road to heaven, for God's 'marvellous lovingkindness' has been shown to me."

So God's lovingkindness may be seen as pardoning great sin; and, next, it may be seen *as delivering from deep trouble*. I may be addressing some poor child of God who is sorely perplexed. These are very trying times, and we constantly meet with godly people, who have a sincere desire to provide things honest in the sight of all men, but who do not find it easy to do so. Some very gracious people have got into a cleft stick; and however they will get out, they cannot imagine. If this is your case, dear friend, I expect you feel very much as John Fawcett's hymn puts it,—

> "My soul, with various tempests toss'd,
> Her hopes o'erturn'd, her projects cross'd,
> Sees every day new straits attend,
> And wonders where the scene will end."

Well, now, if you are ever brought through all your troubles, it will be "marvellous lovingkindness" to you, will it not? Then, go to God with the prayer, "Show me thy marvellous lovingkindness," and he will do it. He will bring you up, and out, and through;—not, perhaps, in the way you would like to come, but he will bring you out in the best way. "Trust in the Lord, and do good; so shalt thou dwell in the land, and verily thou shalt be fed. Delight thyself also in the Lord; and he shall give thee the desires of thine heart. Commit thy way unto the Lord; trust also in him; and he shall bring it to pass." Always expect the unexpected when you are dealing with God. Look to see, in God, and from God, what you never saw before; for the very things, which will seem to unbelief to be utterly impossible, will be those which are most likely to happen when you are dealing with him whose arm is omnipotent, and whose heart is faithful and true. God grant you grace, dear friend, thus to use the prayer of our text as the means of delivering you from deep trouble!

Here is another way to use it. I think you may pray it thus,— at all events, I mean to do so, whether you will or not,—"Lord, reveal thy marvellous lovingkindness to me, *so as to give me high joys and ecstasies of delight.*" I sometimes envy those good people who never go up and never go down, always keeping at one level; theirs must be a very pleasant experience indeed. Still, if ever I do get on the high horse, then I go up far beyond anything I can describe. If ever I do ride upon the clouds, then I do not envy the people who keep along the smooth road. Oh, what deep depressions some of us have had! We have gone down to the very bottoms of the mountains, and the earth with her bars has seemed to be about us for ever; but, after just one glimpse of God's ever-lasting love, we have been up there where the callow lightnings flash, resting and trusting among the tempests, near to God's right hand. I think, nay, I am sure we may pray for this experience. Should not the preacher of the Word wish to know the fulness of love divine? Should not the teacher of the young long to learn all that he can concerning God's infinite love? Though this is the love that passeth knowledge, should not every Christian wish to know all that is knowable of this great love of God? Then let us pray, "Shew thy marvellous lovingkindness." It was truly said, "Thou canst not see God's face, and live;" but I have been inclined to say, "Then, let me see God's face, and die." John Welsh said, when God was flooding his soul with a sense of his wondrous love, "Hold, Lord, hold! I am but an earthen vessel, and thou wilt break me." If I had been there, and I could have borne no more, I would have said, "Do not hold, Lord; break the poor earthen vessel, let it go all to pieces; but anyhow, let thy love be revealed in me!" Oh, that I might even die of this pleasurable pain of knowing too much of God, too much of the ineffable delight of fellowship with him! Let us be very venturesome, beloved, and pray, "Shew thy marvellous lovingkindness."

And, when we have done that, I think we may put up this prayer for ourselves, *as to our own usefulness.* You want to do good, dear brother,—dear sister. Well, then, pray to God, "Show me thy marvellous lovingkindness, O Lord! Use even such a feeble crea-ture as I am. Let heaven, and earth, and hell itself, see that thou canst save souls by poor ignorant men as well as by inspired apostles and learned doctors. Lord, in my chapel, show thy marvellous lovingkindness. Crowd it with people, and bring many of them to Christ. In my class, Lord, show thy marvellous lovingkindness. If there never was a Sunday-school class in which all were saved, Lord, let it be done in mine. Make it a marvellous thing." A dear brother, who prayed at the prayer-meeting before this service, kept on pleading that God would bless me again as he had done before. I liked that prayer; it was as if the friend meant to say to the Lord, "Whatever thou didst in years gone by, do the like over again. If ever it was a marvellous thing to see how the people thronged to hear the Word, Lord, make it more marvellous still." I recollect when some people called our early success "a nine days' wonder." Well, well, well, it has been a good long nine days, anyhow. But, oh, that we might have another nine days like it,—just such another nine days! May God be pleased to send us as many conversions as we had at the first,—ay, and I shall add, and ten times as many! And if ever there have been revivals in the Church of God that have been really marvellous, brothers and sisters, let us take up the cry, "Lord, show thy marvellous loving-kindness again. Send us another Whitefield, and another Wesley, if such will be the kind of men that will bless the world. Send us another Luther, another Calvin, another Zwingle, if such be the men that will bless the world. Lord, send us another Augustine, or another Jerome, if such be the men by whom thou wilt bless the world. But, in some way or other, Lord, show us thy marvellous lovingkindness." "Oh, but!" some would say, "we do not want any excitement. That is an awful thing, you know,—anything like excitement." And, then, perhaps, they add, "We have heard so much of what has been done in previous revivals. It has all ended in smoke, and therefore we really dread the repetition of such an experience." Well, then, brother, you go home, and pray, "Lord, show me thy moderate lovingkindness." When you are on your knees, to-night, pray, "Lord, save half-a-dozen souls here and there.

> " 'We are a garden wall'd around,
> Chosen and made peculiar ground;
> A little spot inclosed by grace
> Out of the world's wide wilderness; '—

"Lord, make it yet smaller, screw us up tighter still, to the glory of thy blessed name!" I don't think any of you can pray that prayer; you shall if you like; but, for my part, I mean to pray, and I hope many of you will join me in it, and may God hear us! "Show us thy marvellous lovingkindness." Oh, for some new miracle of mercy to be wrought in the earth! Oh, for some great thing to be done, such as was done of old! Shall it be so, or not? On this promise it shall depend: "Open thy mouth wide, and I will fill it." But if our mouths be not open, we cannot expect to get the blessing: "According to your faith be it unto you." The Lord grant that our faith may expect to see his "marvellous lovingkindness" displayed yet more and more! Amen and Amen.

7. Christ Is All

" Where there is neither Greek nor Jew, circumcision nor uncircumcision, Barbarian, Scythian, bond nor free : but Christ is all, and in all."—Colossians iii. 11.

PAUL is writing concerning the new creation, and he says that, in it, " There is neither Greek nor Jew, circumcision nor uncircumcision, Barbarian, Scythian, bond nor free: but Christ is all." The new creation is a very different thing from the old one. Blessed are all they who have both seen the kingdom of heaven and entered into it. In the first creation, we are born of the flesh ; and that which is born of the flesh is, even at the best, nothing but flesh, and can never be anything better ; but, in the new creation, we are born of the Spirit, and so we become spiritual, and understand spiritual things. The new life, in Christ Jesus, is an eternal life, and it links all those who possess it with the eternal realities at the right hand of God above.

In some respects, the new creation is so like the old one that a parallel might be drawn between them ; but, in far more respects, it is not at all like the old creation. Many things are absent from the new creation, which were found in the old one; and many things, which were accounted of great value in the first creation, are of little or no worth in the new ; while many distinctions, which were greatly prized in the old creation, are treated as mere insignificant trifles in the new creation. The all-important thing is for each one of us to put to himself or herself the question, " Do I know what it is to have been renewed in knowledge after the image of him who creates anew? Do I know what it is to have been born twice, to have been born again, born from above, by the effectual working of God the Holy Spirit? Do I understand what it is to have spiritually entered a new world wherein dwelleth righteousness?" It is concerning this great truth that I am going to speak ; and, first, I shall say something upon *what is obliterated in the new creation ;* and, secondly, upon *what stands in its stead.*

I. First, as to WHAT IS OBLITERATED IN THE NEW CREATION: "There is neither Greek nor Jew, circumcision nor uncircumcision, Barbarian, Scythian, bond nor free."

That is to say, first, in the kingdom of Christ, *there is an obliteration of all national distinctions.* I suppose there will always be national distinctions, in the world, until Christ comes, even if they should all be terminated then. The mischief was wrought when men tried to build the city and tower, in the plain of Shinar, and so brought Babel, or confusion into the world. The one family became transformed into many,—a necessary evil to prevent a still greater one. The unity at Babel would have been far worse than the confusion has ever been, just as the spiritual union of Babylon, that is, Rome, the Papal system, has been infinitely more mischievous, to the Church and to the world, than the division of Christians into various sects and parties could ever have been. Babel has not been an altogether unmitigated evil; it has, no doubt, wrought a certain amount of good, and prevented colossal streams of evil from reaching a still more awful culmination. Still, the separation is, in itself, an evil; and it is, therefore, in the Lord's own time and way, to be done away with; and, spiritually, it is already abolished. In the Church of Christ, wherever there is real union of heart among believers, nationality is no hindrance to true Christian fellowship. I feel just as much love toward any brother or sister in Christ, who is not of our British race, as I do toward our own Christian countrymen and countrywomen; indeed, I sometimes think I feel even more the force of the spiritual union when I catch the Swiss tone, or the French, or the German, breaking out in the midst of the English, as we often do here, thank God. I seem to feel all the more interest in these beloved brethren and sisters because of the little difference in nationality that there is between us. Certainly, brethren, in any part of the true Church of Christ, all national distinctions are swept away, and we "are no more strangers and foreigners, but fellow-citizens with the saints, and of the household of God."

Under the Christian dispensation, the distinction or division of nationality has gone from us in this sense. We once had our national heroes; each nation still glories in its great men of the heroic age, or in its mythical heroes; but the one Champion and Hero of Christianity is our Lord Jesus Christ, who has slain our dragon foes, routed all our adversaries, broken down the massive fortress of our great enemy, and set the captives free. We sing no longer of the valiant deeds of our national heroes,—St. George, St. Andrew, St. Patrick, St. Denis, and the other " saints " so-called, who were either only legendary, or else anything but " saints " as we understand the term. We sing the prowess of the King of all saints, the mighty Son of David, who is worthy of our loftiest minstrelsy. King Arthur and the knights of the round table, we are quite willing to forget when we think of " another King, one Jesus," and of another table, where they who sit are not merely good knights of Jesus Christ, but are made kings and priests unto him who sits at the head of the festal board. Barbarian, Scythian,

Greek, Jew,—these distinctions are all gone so far as we are concerned, for we are all one in Christ Jesus. We boast not of our national or natural descent, or of the heroes whose blood may be in our veins; it is enough for us that Christ has lived, and Christ has died, and Christ has "spoiled principalities and powers," and trampled down sin, death, and hell, even as he fell amid the agonies of Calvary.

Away, too, has gone all our national history, so far as there may have been any desire to exalt it for the purpose of angering Christian brethren and sisters of another race. I wish that even the names of wars and famous battlefields could be altogether forgotten; but if they do remain in the memories of those of us who are Christians, we will not boast as he did who said, " But 'twas a famous victory;" nor will we proudly sing of—

" The flag that braved a thousand years
The battle and the breeze."

As Christians, our true history begins—nay, I must correct myself, for it had no beginning except in that dateless eternity when the Divine Trinity in Unity conceived the wondrous plan of predestinating grace, electing love, the substitutionary sacrifice of the Son of God for the sins of his chosen people, the full and free justification of all who believe, and the eternal glory of the whole redeemed family of God. This is our past, present, and future history; we, who are Christians, take down the Volume of the Book wherein these things are written, and we make our boast in the Lord, and thus the boasting is not sinful.

As to laws and customs, of which each nation has its own, it is not wrong for a Christian to take delight in a good custom which has been long established, or earnestly to contend for the maintenance of ancient laws, which have preserved inviolate the liberty of the people age after age; but, still, the customs of Christians are learned from the example of Christ, and the laws of believers are the precepts laid down by him. When we are dealing with matters relating to the Church of Christ, we have no English customs, or French customs, or American customs, or German customs; or, if we have, we should let them go, and have only Christian customs henceforth. Did our Lord Jesus Christ command anything? Then, let it be done. Did he forbid anything? Then, away with it. Would he smile upon a certain action? Then, perform it at once. Would he frown upon it? Then, mind that you do the same. Blessed is the believer who has realized that the laws and customs for the people of God to observe are plainly written out in the life of Christ, and that he has become to us, now, " all, and in all."

Christ, by giving liberty to all his people, has also obliterated the distinctions of nationality which we once located in various countries. One remembers, with interest, the old declaration, " *Romanus sum*," (" I am a Roman,") for a citizen of Rome, wherever he might be, felt that he was a free man whom none would dare to hurt, else Roman legions would ask the reason why; and an Englishman, in every country, wherever he may be, still feels that he is one who was born free, and who would sooner die than become a slave, or hold another man or woman in slavery. But, brethren and sisters, there is a higher liberty than this,—the liberty wherewith Christ has made his people free; and when we come into the Church of God, we talk about that liberty, and we believe that Christians, even if they had not the civil and religious rights which we possess, would still be as free in Christ as we are. There are still many, in various parts of the world, who do not enjoy the liberties that we have; who, notwithstanding their bonds, are spiritually free; for, as the Son hath made them free, they are free indeed.

Christ also takes from us all inclination or power to boast of our national prestige. To me, it is prestige enough to be a Christian;— to bear the cross Christ gives me to carry, and to follow in the footsteps of the great Cross-bearer. What is the power, in which some boast, of sending soldiers and cannon to a distant shore, compared with the almighty power wherewith Christ guards the weakest of us who dares to trust him? What reason is there for a man to be lifted up with conceit just because he happens to have been born in this or that highly-favoured country? What is such a privilege compared with the glories which appertain to the man who is born again from above, who is an heir of heaven, a child of God through faith in Jesus Christ, and who can truthfully say, " All things are mine, and I am Christ's, and Christ is God's "?

What is the wondrous internationalism that levels all these various nationalities in the Church of Christ, and makes us all one in him? Spiritually, we have all been born in one country; the New Jerusalem is the mother of us all. It is not my boast that I am a citizen of this or that earthly city or town here; it is my joy that I am one of the citizens of " a city which hath foundations, whose Builder and Maker is God." Christ has fired all of us, who are his people, with a common enthusiasm. He has revealed himself to each one of us as he doth not unto the world; and, in the happy remembrance that we belong to him, we forget that we are called by this or that national name, and only remember that he is our Lord, and that we are to follow where he leads the way. He has pointed us to heaven, as the leader of the Goths and Huns pointed his followers to Italy, and said, " There is the country whence come the luscious wines of which you have tasted. Go, and take the vineyards, and grow the vines for yourselves;" and so they forgot that they belonged to various tribes, and they all united under the one commander who promised to lead them on to the conquest of the rich land for which they panted. And now, we, who are in Christ Jesus, having tasted of the Eshcol clusters which grow in the heavenly Canaan, follow our glorious Leader and Commander, as the Israelites followed Joshua, forgetting that we belong to so many different tribes, but knowing that there is an inheritance reserved in heaven for all who follow where Jehovah-Jesus leads the way.

The next thing to be observed, in our text, is that *ceremonial distinctions are obliterated*. When Paul says that " there is neither circumcision nor uncircumcision," he recalls the fact that, under the law, there were some who were peculiarly the children of promise, to whom were committed the oracles of God; but there is no such thing as that now. Then there were others, who stood outside the pale of the law,—the sinners of the Gentiles, who were left in darkness until their time for receiving the light should come; but Christ has fused these two into one; and, now, in his Church, "there is neither Greek nor Jew." I marvel at the insanity of those who try to prove that we are Jews,—the lost ten tribes, forsooth! I grant you that the business transactions of a great many citizens of London afford some support to the theory, but it is only a theory, and a very crazy one, too. But suppose they were able to prove that we are of the seed of Abraham, after the flesh, it would not make any difference to us, for we are expressly told that "there is neither Greek nor Jew, circumcision nor uncircumcision," for all believers are one in Christ Jesus. The all-important consideration is,—Are we Christians? Do we really believe in Jesus Christ, to the salvation of our souls? The apostle truly says, "Christ is all," for he has done away with all the distinctions that formerly existed between Jews and Gentiles. He has levelled down and he has levelled up. First he has levelled down the Jews, and made them stand in the same class as the Gentiles, shutting them up under the custody of the very law in which they gloried, and making them see that they can never come out of that bondage except by using the key of faith in Christ. So our Lord Jesus has stopped the mouths of both Jews and Gentiles, and made them stand equally guilty before God; for, on the other hand, he has levelled up the outcast and despised Gentiles, and has admitted us to all the privileges of his ancient covenant, making us to be heirs of Abraham, in a spiritual sense, "though Abraham be ignorant of us, and Israel acknowledge us not." He has given to us all the blessings which belong to Abraham's seed, because we, too, possess like precious faith as the father of the faithful himself had. So, "now in Christ Jesus we who sometimes were far off are made nigh by the blood of Christ. For he is our peace, who hath made both one, and hath broken down the middle wall of partition between us; having abolished in his flesh the enmity, even the law of commandments contained in ordinances; for to make in himself of twain one new man, so making peace." Oh, what a blessing it is that all national and ceremonial distinctions are gone for ever, and that "Christ is all" to all who believe in him!

A more difficult point, perhaps, is that of *social distinctions;* but that also has gone from the Church of Christ. "There is neither bond nor free," says the apostle. Well, blessed be God, slavery has almost ceased to exist. Among Christians, it has become a by-word and a proverb, though there was a time when some of them pleaded for it as a divinely-ordained institution. But, oh, may the last vestige of it speedily disappear, and may every man see it to be both his duty and his privilege to yield to his brother-man his God-given rights and liberties! Yet, even in such a free country as ours happily is, there are still distinctions between one class and another, and I expect there always will be. I do not suppose there ever can be, in this world, any system, even if we could have the profoundest philosophers to invent it, in which everybody will be equal. Or, if they ever should be all equal, they would not remain so for more than five minutes. We are not all equal in our form, and shape, and capacity, and ability; and we never shall be. We could not have the various members of our body all equal; if we had such an arrangement as that, our body would be a monstrosity. There are some members of the body which must have a more honourable office and function than others have; but all the members are in the body, and necessary to its due proportion. So is it in the Church of Christ, which is his mystical body; yet, brethren, how very, very minute are the distinctions between the various members of that body! You, my brother, are rich, as the world reckons riches. Well, do not boast of your wealth, for riches are very apt to take to themselves wings, and fly away. Probably, more of you are poor so far as worldly wealth is concerned. Well, then, do not murmur, for " all things are yours " if you are Christ's; and, soon, you will be where you will know nothing of poverty again for ever and ever. True Christianity practically wipes out all these distinctions by saying, " This man, as one of Christ's stewards, has more of his Lord's money entrusted to him than others have, so he is bound to do more with it than they do with their portion; he must give away more than they do." This other man has far less than his rich brother, but Christ says that he is responsible for the right use of what he hath, and not for what he hath not. As the poor widow's two mites drop into the treasury of the Lord, he receives her gift with as sweet a smile as that which he accorded to the lavish gifts of David and Solomon. In his Church, Christ teaches us that, if we have more than others, we simply hold it in trust for those who have less than we have; and I believe that some of the Lord's children are poor in order that there may be an opportunity for their fellow-Christians to minister to them out of their abundance. We could not prove our devotion to Christ, in practical service such as he best loves, if there were not needy ones whom we could succour and support. Our Lord has told us how he will say, in the great day of account, " I was an hungred, and ye gave me meat;" but that could not be the case if there was not one of the least of his brethren, who was hungry, and whom we could feed for his sake. " I was thirsty, and ye gave me drink." But he could not say that if none of his poor brethren were thirsty. " I was sick, and ye visited me." So, there must be sick saints to be visited, and cases of distress, of various kinds, to be relieved; otherwise, there could not be the opportunity of practically proving our love to our Lord. In the Church of Christ, it ought always to be so, brethren; we should love each other with a pure heart fervently; we should bear each other's burdens, and so fulfil the law of Christ; and we should care for one another, and seek, as far as we can, to supply one another's needs. The rich brother must not exalt himself above the poor one, nor must the poor Christian envy his richer brethren and sisters in Christ; for, in him, all these distinctions are obliterated, and we sit down, at his table, as members of the one family of which he is the glorious and ever-living Head; and we dwell together in unity, praising him that national, ceremonial, and social distinctions have, for us, all passed away, and that " Christ is all, and in all."

II. Possibly, I have taken up too much of our time in describing what is obliterated from the old creation; so, now, I will try more briefly to show you WHAT TAKES ITS PLACE IN THE NEW CREATION: " Christ is all, and in all."

First, *Christ is all our culture.* Has Christianity wiped out that grand name " Greek "? Yes, in the old meaning of it; and, in some senses, it is a great pity that it is gone, for the Greek was a cultured man, the Greek's every movement was elegance itself, the Greek was the standard of classic beauty and eloquence; but Christianity has wiped all that out, and written, in its place, " Christ is all." And, brethren, the culture, the gracefulness, the beauty, the comeliness, the eloquence,—in the sight of the best Judge of all those things, namely, God, the ever-blessed,—which Christ gives to the true Christian, is better than all that Greek art or civilization ever produced, so we may cheerfully let it all go, and say, " Christ is all."

Next, *Christ is all our revelation.* There was the " Jew ";—he was a fine fellow, and there is still much to admire in him. The Semitic race seems to have been specially constituted by God for devout worship; and the Jew, the descendant of believing Abraham, is still a firm believer in one part of God's Word; he is, spiritually, a staunch Conservative in that matter, the very backbone of the world's belief. Alas, that his faith is so incomplete, and that there is mingled with it so much tradition received from his fathers! Will you wipe out that name " Jew "? Yes, because we, who believe in Jesus, glory in him even as the Jew gloried in having received the oracles of God. Christ is " the Word of God " incarnate, and all the divine revelation is centered in him; and we hold fast the eternal verities which have been committed unto us, because of the power of Christ that rests upon us.

Then, next, *Christ is all our ritual.* There is no " circumcision " now. That was the special mark of those who were separated from all the rest of mankind; they bore in their body undoubted indications that they were set apart to be the Lord's peculiar possession. Someone asks, " Will you do away with that distinguishing rite? " Yes, we will; for, in Christ, every true Christian is set apart unto God, marked as Jesus Christ's special separated one by the circumcision made without hands.

Further, *Christ is all our simplicity.* Here is a man, who says that " uncircumcision " is his distinguishing mark, and adds, " I am not separated or set apart from others, as the so-called ' priest ' is; I am a man among my fellow-men. Wherever I go, I can mingle with others, and feel that they are my brethren. I belong to the ' uncircumcision.' Will you rule that out? " Yes, we will, because we have, in Christ, all that uncircumcision means; for he who becomes a real Christian is the truest of all men; he is the most free from that spirit which says, "Stand by thyself, come not near to me; for I am holier than thou." He is the true philanthropist, the real lover of men, even as Christ was. He was no separatist, in the sense in which some use that word. He went to a wedding feast; he ate bread in the house of a publican; and a woman of the city, who was a sinner, was permitted to wash his feet with her tears. He mingled with the rest of mankind, and " the common people heard him gladly;" and he would have us to be as he was, the true Man among men, the great Lover of our race.

Once more, *Christ is all our natural traditions, and our uncon-querableness and liberty.* Here is " the rude barbarian ", as the poet calls him; he says, "I shall never give up the free, manly life that I have lived so long. By my unshorn beard," for that is the meaning of the term Barbarian, "I swear it shall be so." " By the wild steppes and wide plains, over which I roam unconquerable," says the Scythian, " I will never bend to the conventionalities of civilization, and be the slave of your modern luxuries." Well, it is almost a pity to have done with Barbarians and Scythians, in this sense, for there is a good deal about them to be commended; but we must wipe them all out. If they come into the Church of Christ, he must be " all, and in all;" because everything that is manly, everything that is natural, everything that is free, everything that is bold, everything that is unconquerable will be put into them if " Christ is all " to them. They will get all the excellences that are in that freedom, without the faults appertaining to it.

Further, "*Christ is all*" *as our Master, if we be* "*bond.*" I think I see, in the great assembly at Colosse, which Paul addressed, one who said, " But I am a bond slave; a man bought me at the auction mart, and here, on my back, are the marks of the slave-holder's lash." And I think I hear him add, " I wish that disgrace could be wiped out." But Paul says, " Brother, it *is* wiped out; you are no bond slave, really, for Christ has made you free." Then the great apostle of the Gentiles comes, and sits down by his side, and says to him, " The Church of Christ has absorbed you, brother, by making us all like you; for we are all servants of one Master; and look," says Paul, as he bares his own back, and shows the scars from his repeated scourgings, " from henceforth let no man trouble me, for I bear in my body the marks of the Lord Jesus." " And so," says he, laying his hand on the poor Christian slave, " I, Paul, the slave of Jesus Christ, share your servitude, and with me you are Christ's free man."

Lastly, *Christ is our Magna Charta; yea, our liberty itself if we be* "*free.*" Here comes the free man, who was born free. Shall that clause stand, " neither bond nor free"? Oh, yes, let it stand; but not so stand that we glory in our national freedom, for Christ has given us a higher freedom. I may slightly alter the familiar couplet, and say,—

" He is the free man whom THE LORD makes free,
And all are slaves beside."

Oh, what multitudes of people, in London, are slaves;—miserable slaves to the opinions of their neighbours,—slaves to the caprice of Mrs. Grundy,—slaves to "respectability"! Some of you dare not do a thing that you know to be right, because somebody might make a remark about it. What are you but slaves? Ay, and there are slaves in the pulpit, every Sunday, who dare not speak the truth for fear somebody should be offended; and there are also slaves in the pews, and slaves in the shops, and slaves all around. What a wretched life a slave lives! Yet, till you become a Christian, and know what it is to wear Christ's bonds about your willing wrists, you will always feel the galling fetters of society, and the bonds of custom, fashion, or this or that. But Jesus makes us free with a higher freedom, so we wipe out the mere terrestrial freedom, which is too often only a sham, and we write, "Christ is all."

So, to conclude, remember that, if you have Christ as your Saviour, you do not need anybody else to save you. I see an old gentleman, over there in Rome, with a triple crown on his head. We do not want him, for "Christ is all." He says that he is the vicegerent of God; that is not true; but if it were, it would not matter, for "Christ is all," so we can do without the Pope. Then I see another gentleman, with an all-round dog collar of the Roman kennel type; and he tells me that, if I will confess my sins to him as the priest of the parish, he can give me absolution; but, seeing that "Christ is all," we can do without that gentleman as well as the other one; for anything that is over and above "all" must be a superfluity, if nothing worse. So is it with everything that is beside or beyond Christ; faith can get to Christ without Pope or priest. Everything that is outside Christ is a lie, for "Christ is all." All that is true must be inside him, so we can do without all others in the matter of our soul's salvation.

But supposing that we have not received Christ as our Saviour, then how unspeakably poor we are! If we have not grasped Christ by faith, we have not laid hold of anything, for "Christ is all;" and if we have not him who is all, we have nothing at all. "Oh!" says one, "I am a regular chapel-goer." Yes; so far, so good; but if you have not Christ, you have nothing, for "Christ is all." "But I have been baptized," says another. Ah! but if you have not savingly trusted in Christ, your baptism is only another sin added to all your others. "But I go to communion," says another. So much the worse for you if you have not trusted in Christ as your Saviour. I wish I could put this thought into the heart of everyone here who is without Christ,—nay, I pray the Holy Spirit to impress this thought upon your heart,—if you are without Christ, you are without everything that is worth having, for "Christ is all."

But, Christians, I would like to make your hearts dance by reminding you that, if you have Christ as your Saviour, you are rich to all the intents of bliss, for you have "all" that your heart can wish to have. Nobody else can say as much as that; the richest man in the world has only got something, though the something may be very great. Alexander conquered one world; but you, believer, in getting Christ as yours, have this world and also that which is to come, life and death, time and eternity. Oh, revel in the thought that, as Christ is yours, you are rich to an infinity of riches, for " Christ is all."

Now, if Christ really is yours, and as Christ is all, then love him, and honour him, and praise him. Mother, what were you doing this afternoon? Pressing that dear child of yours to your bosom, and saying, " She is my all "? Take back those words, for they are not true. If you love Christ, he is your all, and you cannot have another " all." Someone else has one who is very near and very dear. If you are that someone else, and you have said in your heart, " He is my all," or " She is my all," you have done wrong, for nothing and no one but Christ must be your " all." You will be an idolater, and you will grieve the Holy Spirit, if anything, or anyone, except Christ, becomes your " all." You, who have lately lost your loved ones, and you, who have been brought low by recent losses in business, are you fretting over your losses? If so, remember that you have not lost your " all." You still have Christ, and he is " all." Then, what have you lost? Yes, I know that you have something to grieve over; but, after all, your " light affliction, which is but for a moment, worketh for you a far more exceeding and eternal weight of glory;" therefore, comfort yourself with this thought,—" I have not really lost anything, for I still have all." When you have all things, find Christ in all; and when you have lost all things, then find all things in Christ. I do not know, but I think that the latter is the better of the two.

Now, if Christ be all, then, beloved brethren and sisters, let us live for him. If he is all, let us spend our strength, and be ready to lay down the last particle of it that we have, and to die for him; and then let us, whenever we need anything, go to him for it, for " Christ is all." Let us draw upon this bank, for its resources are infinite; we shall never exhaust them.

Lastly, and chiefly, let us send our hearts right on to where he is. Where our treasure is, there should our hearts be also. Come, my heart, up and away! What hast thou here that can fill thee? What hast thou here that can satisfy thee? Plume thy wings, and be up and away, for there is thy roosting-place; there is the tree of life which never can be felled. Up and away, and build there for ever! The Lord help each one of you to do so, for Jesus' sake! Amen.

8. A Blessed Gospel Chain

"Jesus answered and said unto him, If a man love me, he will keep my words: and my Father will love him, and we will come unto him, and make our abode with him."—John xiv. 23.

THIS is a blessed chain of gospel experience. Our text is not meant for the men of the world, who have their portion in this life, but for the chosen, and called, and faithful, who are brought into the inner circle of Christ's disciples, and taught to understand the mysteries of his kingdom. It was in answer to the question of Jude as to how Christ would manifest himself to his own, and not to the world, that these words were spoken, and Christ explained that it would be manifest who were his own people by certain marks and signs. They would be those who love him, and keep his commandments, and so win the complacency of the Father; and the Father and the Son would come to these loving and obedient disciples, and make their abode with them. God grant that all of us may be able to take each of the steps here mentioned, so that our Lord may manifest himself to us as he does not unto the world!

The subject upon which I am about to speak to you is one which the preacher cannot handle without the people. I must have God's people with me in spirit to help me while I am dealing with such a topic as this. You know that, in the Church of England service, there are certain places where the clergyman says, " saying after me," so that it is not simply the minister alone uttering the prayer or the confession, but he is a sort of precentor leading the rest of the congregation. In a similar style, I want you people of God, as the Holy Spirit shall enable you, to bend all your thoughts and energies in this direction, and step by step to climb with me to these distinct spiritual platforms,—ascending from the one to the other by the Spirit's gracious aid, that your fellowship may be with the Father, and with his Son, Jesus Christ.

I. Our text begins with the first link in this golden chain, namely, LOVE TO CHRIST : " If a man love me."

This " if " seems to me to stand at the portals of our text, like a sentinel at the gate of a palace, to prevent anybody from entering who ought not to enter. It is an " if " that may be passed round the present assembly, for I fear that all in this house do not love the Lord Jesus Christ. If you cannot answer in the affirmative the question asked by the lips of Jesus himself, " Lovest thou me? " you have nothing to do with the rest of this verse. Indeed, what have you to do with any of the privileges revealed in the Bible, or with any of the blessings promised there, so long as you are without love to Christ? Let that " if " stand, then, as with a drawn sword, like the cherubim at the gate of the garden of Eden, to keep you from venturing to intrude where you have no right to go if you do not love the Lord Jesus Christ : " *If* a man love me."

Art thou a lover of the Lord, dear hearer? Put not that question aside, but answer it honestly, in his sight, for *there are some, who only pretend to love him*, but really do not ;—some, who make a loud profession, but their language is hypocritical, for their conduct is not consistent therewith. Do *you* love the Lord Jesus with your whole heart? He is well worthy of your love, so let the question go round the whole assembly, and not miss any one of us, " Lovest thou me? "

For there are some, too, who are *Christ's disciples only by profession*. All they give him is a cold-hearted assent to his teaching. Their head is convinced, and, in a measure, their life is not altogether inconsistent with their profession ; but their heart is dead ; or, if it be at all alive, it is like that of the church of Laodicea, neither cold nor hot, but lukewarm ; and that is a state which Christ abhors. He must occupy the throne of our hearts, and be the best loved of all, or else we lack that which is essential to true Christianity.

" If a man love me," says Christ ; so, do you love him? I do not ask whether you love his offices, though I hope you do. You love the Prophet, the Priest, the King, the Shepherd, the Saviour, and whatsoever other title he assumes ; each of these names is music to your ear ;—but do you love Christ himself? I will not ask whether you love his work, especially the great redemption which comprehends such innumerable blessings. I hope you do ; but it is a personal love to Christ that is spoken of here. Jesus says, " If any man love *me*." Have you realized Christ, personally, as still alive, and gone into heaven, and soon to come again in all the glory of his Father and of the holy angels? Say, brother, sister, dost thou love *him?* " If," says Christ, " If a man love me," so it is right and wise for each one of us to put that question to ourselves, even though we know that we can answer it satisfactorily, and say,—

> " Yes, I love thee, and adore ;
> Oh, for grace to love thee more ! "

And if there should be any doubt about the matter, we ought to put the question, pointedly, again, and again, and again, and let not ourselves escape till there is a definite answer given one way or another. Heart of mine, dost thou really love the Saviour? Brothers and sisters, put this question to yourselves; and if you do love him, let your love well up like a mighty geyser,—the hot spring that leaps up to a great height. So let the hot spring of your love to Jesus leap up now, and let each one of you say to him,—

> "My Jesus, I love thee, I know thou art mine,
> For thee all the follies of sin I resign ;
> My gracious Redeemer, my Saviour art thou,
> If ever I loved thee, my Jesus, 'tis now."

If you can do so, then you may add,—

> "I will love thee in life, I will love thee in death,
> And praise thee as long as thou lendest me breath ;
> And say when the death-dew lies cold on my brow,
> If ever I loved thee, my Jesus, 'tis now."

Remember that, *if you do love him, he must have loved you first.* Think of his ancient love,—the love that was fixed upon you or ever the earth was, when he saw you in the glass of futurity, and beheld all that you would be in the ruinous fall of Adam, and by your own personal transgression, and yet loved you, notwithstanding all. Think of him, when the fulness of time was come, stripping himself of all his glory, and descending from the throne of infinite majesty to the manger of humiliation, and being there, as a babe, swaddled in his weakness. Will you not love him who became God incarnate for you? Think of him all through his life,—a life of poverty, for he had not where to lay his head ;—a life of rejection, for " he came unto his own, and his own received him not ;"—a life of pain, for he bare our sicknesses ;—a life of dishonour, for he was despised and rejected of men. Will you further think of him in the garden of Gethsemane? Will not your love be stirred as you watch the bloody sweat, and hear his groans and mark his tears, as he pleads with God until he prevails? Follow him to the judgment-seat, and hear him there charged with sedition and with blasphemy, if you can bear it. Then see the soldiers, as they spit in his face and mock him, while they thrust a reed into his hand for a sceptre, and put on his brow a crown of thorns as his only diadem. See him tied up to be scourged, till the cruel thongs lacerate and tear his precious flesh, and he suffers agonies indescribable. And when you have followed him so far, go further still, and stand at the cross-foot, and mark the crimson stream that flows from his hands, and feet, and side. Stand and watch him when the soldier's spear has pierced his heart, and made the blood and water flow forth for your pardon and cleansing. Did he suffer all this for you, and do you not love him in return? May I not tell that " if " to get out of the way, and let you pass in, that you may take the next step? Track him as he rises from the grave for you, as he ascends to heaven for you, and obtains great gifts for you ; and as yonder, before his Father's face, he pleads for you ; and as there he governs all things, as King of kings, and Lord of lords, and governs all for you; as there he prepares many mansions for his own people; and as there he gets ready to come to earth, the second time, that he may receive his people unto himself, that where he is they may be also for ever and for evermore. As you think of all this, love the Lord, ye who are his saints, ye who have been washed in his blood, love him! Ye who are wearing the spotless robe of his righteousness,—love him. Ye who call him " Husband ", love him,—ye who are married to him,—united in bonds that can never be severed.

II. If this be true of you, let us pass on to the next point, that of KEEPING CHRIST'S WORDS. "If any man love me," says Christ, " he will keep my words." Let us see how far we have kept his words.

I trust that, first, we keep his words *by treasuring them, and prizing them.* Brothers and sisters, I hope that we venerate every word that Christ has ever uttered. I trust that we desire to treasure up every syllable that he has ever spoken. There is not a word of his, recorded in the Gospels, or in any other of the inspired pages of revelation, by which we do not set more store than by much fine gold.

I trust that we keep Christ's words, next, by *trying to know them.* Are you all diligent students of the Word? Do you search the Scriptures? Do you live upon the truth that the Lord hath spoken? You should do so, for every word that cometh out of his mouth is the true food of your souls. I must ask you whether you are doing these two things. Are you keeping Christ's words by prizing them, and by seeking to be so familiar with them that you know what his words are?

Then, next, do you endeavour to lift the latch, and *to find your way into the inner meaning of his words?* Do you pierce the shell to get at the kernel? Does the Spirit of God lead you into all truth, or are you content with the rudiments of the faith? This is the way to keep Christ's words, namely, by endeavouring, to your very utmost, to understand what the meaning of those words may be.

Then, when you know the meaning of them, *do you seek to keep them in your hearts?* Do you love what Christ has spoken, so that you delight to know what it is, and love it because it is his doctrine? Will you sit at his feet, and receive the instruction that he is willing to impart? Have you attained to that stage that you even love his rebukes? If his words come home to you, and sharply reprove you, do you love them even then, and lay bare your heart before him that you may feel more and more the faithful wounds of this your beloved Friend? Do you also love his precepts? Are they as sweet to you as his promises; or, if you could do as you wish, would you cut them out of the Bible, and get rid of them? O brothers and sisters, it is a blessed proof that grace has been largely given to us when even the smallest word uttered by Jesus Christ is more precious to us than all the diamonds in the world, and we feel that we only want to know what he has said, and to love whatever he has spoken.

"If a man love me, he will keep my words." This declaration of our Lord suggests this question,—*Do we keep his words practically?* That is a most important point, for you will not be able to get any further if you stumble here. Do you endeavour, in a practical way, to keep all his moral precepts? Are you trying to be, in your lives, as far as you can, like him; or are you selfish unkind, worldly? Are you endeavouring to be like him who hath left you an example that you should follow in his steps? Come, answer honestly. Is this the object of your being? Are you seeking to be moulded by the Holy Spirit in that way? And are you practically keeping Christ's words as to the precepts of the gospel? Have you believed on him? Believing on him, have you been baptized according to his command? Being baptized, do you come to his table, according to his bidding, "This do in remembrance of me"? Or do you turn on your heel, and say that these are non-essential things?

Beloved, if your heart is right with God, you will want to know all his words, and to put them into practice. What care I about the words of any earthly church? They are only the words of men; but search ye, and find the words of Christ; and wherever they lead you, even though you are the only one who has ever been led in that way, follow wherever he leads. You cannot take the next step mentioned in my text unless you can deliberately say, "Yes, Lord, 'thy words were found, and I did eat them; and thy word was unto me the joy and rejoicing of mine heart; for I am called by thy name, O Lord God of hosts;' and I long to walk in all thy statutes and ordinances, blamelessly, even to the end of my days." You may err; you may make mistakes; you may commit sin; but the intent of your heart must be that, having loved the Lord, you will keep his words in those various senses that I have mentioned.

III. If you have been enabled to pass through these two gates, you may now come to the next one, which tells us of A HIGH PRIVILEGE AND GREAT JOY: "He will keep my words, and *my Father will love him.*"

What wonderful words these are,—"My Father will love him"! It is quite certain that he will do so; for, when a man loves Jesus, he is in sympathy with the Eternal Father himself. You know, my brethren, that the Father's love is fixed upon his only-begotten Son. One with himself in his essential Deity, he has loved him from eternity; but since Jesus has been obedient unto death, "even the death of the cross," we cannot imagine what must be the Father's complacency in the blessed person of our risen and ascended Lord. This is a deep subject, and there is no human mind that can ever fathom the depths of it, and tell how truly and how wonderfully the Father loves his everlasting Son. So, you see, brethren, that, if we love Jesus Christ, our heart meets the heart of God, for the Father also loves him. Have you never felt, when you have been trying to praise Jesus, that you are doing, in your feeble way, just what God has always been doing in his own infinite way? The ever-blessed Spirit is continually glorifying Jesus; and when you are doing the same, God and you, though with very unequal footsteps, are treading the same path, and are in sympathy the one with the other.

Then, besides the fact that you are in sympathy with the Father in having one object of love, you are also in sympathy with him as to character. Jesus said, " If a man love me, he will keep my words." Well, when you are keeping Christ's words,—when the Divine Spirit is making you obedient to Jesus, and like to Jesus,— you are treading the path where your Heavenly Father would have you walk, and therefore he loves you.

Let me make a clear distinction here. I am not now speaking about the general love of God towards all mankind,—that love of benevolence and beneficence which is displayed even towards the thankless and the evil. Neither am I speaking, just now, concerning the essential love of God towards his own elect, whom he loves, irrespectively of their character, because of his own sovereign choice of them from eternity; but I am speaking of that complacent love which God, as a Father, has towards his own children. You know that you often say to your child, " If you do this or that, your father will love you;" yet you know that a father will love his child, as his child, and always must do so even if his character is not all that the father desires it to be. But what a love that is which a father has to a good, dutiful, obedient child! It is a love of which he talks to him again and again, a love which he manifests to him in many sweet and kindly words, a love which he displays to him in many actions which he would not otherwise have done, bestowing upon him many favours which it would not have been safe to bestow upon him if he had been a naughty, disobedient child. Never forget that our Heavenly Father exercises wise discipline in his house. He has rods for his children who disobey him, and he has smiles for his children who keep his commands. If we walk contrary to him, he has told us that he will walk contrary to us; but if our ways please him, there are many choice favours which he bestows upon us. This teaching is not suggestive of legal bondage, for we are not under law, but under grace; but this is the law of God's house under the rule of grace;—for instance, if a man keeps the Lord's commandments, he will have power with God in prayer; but when a man lives habitually in sin, or even occasionally falls into sin, he cannot pray so as to prevail, he cannot win the ear of God as he used to do. You know right well that, if you have offended the Lord in any way, you cannot enjoy the gospel as you did before you so sinned. The Bible, instead of smiling upon you, seems to threaten you, in every text and every line; it seems to rise up, as in letters of fire, and burn its way into your conscience.

It is certainly true that the Lord deals differently with his own children according to their condition and character. So, when a man is brought into such a state of heart that he keeps Christ's words, then his character is of such a kind that God can take a complacent delight in him, and in this sense can love him. It is in such a case as this that the Father will let us know that he loves us, that he will assure us of that love, and shed it abroad in our hearts by the Holy Ghost. He will give us special blessings, perhaps in providence, but certainly in grace. He will give us special joy and rejoicing; our horn shall be exalted, and our feet shall stand upon the high places of the earth. All things—even his trials—shall be blessed to the man who walks aright with God; and the way to do that is to love Christ, and to keep his words. Of such a man, Jesus says, "My Father will love him."

IV. If you have passed through these three gates, you come to another which bears this inscription, "WE WILL COME UNTO HIM."

This is a singular use of the plural pronoun: "*We* will come unto him." It is a proof of the distinct personality of the Father and of the Son. Jesus says, "If a man love me," (do not forget the previous links in this blessed gospel chain,) "he will keep my words: and my Father will love him;" and then follows this gracious assurance: "We will come unto him." Does not this mean, first, *distance removed?* There is no longer a gap between such a man's soul and his God. He feels heavy in heart, perhaps, and thinks, "I cannot get near to God;" but he hears this comforting message, "We will come unto him;" and, soon, over all the mountains of division that there may have been in the past, like a roe, or a young hart, the Well-beloved comes; and the great Father, when he sees, in the distance, his child returning to him, runs to meet him, and folds him to his heart. What a wondrous divine coming this is! Christ and his Father, by the Holy Spirit, come to pay the believer a most gracious visit. Yes, beloved, if you are living in love to Christ, and keeping his words, there will not be any distance separating you from the Father and the Son, but the text will be blessedly fulfilled in your experience, "We will come unto him."

And, while it means distance removed, it also means *honour conferred.* Many a great nobleman has beggared himself that he might receive a prince or a king into his house; the entertainment of royalty has meant the mortgaging of his estates; that is a poor return for the honour of receiving a visit from his sovereign. But, behold, my brothers and sisters, how different it is with us. The obedient lover of the Lord Jesus Christ has the Father and the Son to visit him, and he is greatly enriched by their coming. He may be very poor, but Jesus says, "We will come unto him." He may be obscure and illiterate, but Jesus says, "We will come unto him." Do you all, dear friends, know what this coming means? Did you ever know the Son to come to you with his precious blood applied to your conscience, till you realized that every one of your sins was forgiven? Have you taken Jesus up in your arms, spiritually, as old Simeon did literally, and said, with him, "Lord, now lettest thou thy servant depart in peace according to thy word, for mine eyes have seen thy salvation"? Has Jesus seemed, to your faith, to be as near to you as one who sat on the same chair with you, and talked with you in most familiar conversation? It has been so with some of us, and it has often been so.

This also has meant *knowledge increased.* Jesus has revealed himself to us by coming to us, even as he came to the two disciples on the way to Emmaus. Then, in addition, have you not known the Father come to you, in his Divine relationship, yet making you feel yourself his child, and causing you to realize that he loved you as truly as you love your own children, only much more deeply and fervently than human love can ever be? Have you not received, at his hands, such tokens for good, and such benedictions as only he could give, so that you felt the Divine Fatherhood to be something coming very near to you, and the Spirit of God, operating within you, has made you cry, "Abba, Father," with an unstammering tongue? "We will come unto him." The Saviour will come, and the Father will come, and the blessed Spirit will represent them both in the believer's heart.

So, "We will come unto him," means distance removed, honour conferred, and knowledge increased; and it also means *assistance brought;* for, if the Father and the Son come to us, what more can we need? With their gracious presence in our souls, we have omnipotence and omniscience, infinity and all-sufficiency, on our side, and grace to help us in every time of need.

V. The last clause of the text, and the sweetest of all, is, "AND MAKE OUR ABODE WITH HIM."

Can you catch the full meaning of that phrase? Jesus says that the Father and the Son will visit us; they will come to us, as the three blessed ones came to Abraham when he was at the tent door, and he entertained the Lord and his attendant angels; but they did not make their abode with him. They went on their way, and Abraham was left in the plains of Mamre. God often visited Abraham, and spake familiarly with him, but our Saviour's promise goes beyond that; he says, "We will come unto him, and make our *abode* with him." To make your abode with a person, is for that person and yourself to have the same house and home, and to live together. In this case, it means that the Lord will make his people to be his temple wherein he will dwell continually. "We will come unto him, and make our abode with him." I have turned that thought over and over again until I have got the sweetness of it into my own heart; but I cannot communicate it to your minds and hearts; only the Holy Spirit can do that.

See what this expression means. *What knowledge of one another is implied here!* Do you want to know a person? You must live with him; you do not really know anybody, however much you may think you know, until you have done so. But, oh, if the Father and the Son come and live with us, we shall know them,—know the Father and the Son! This is not the portion of carnal minds; neither is it for professing Christians who have not fulfilled the conditions laid down by our Lord; but it is for those who love Christ, and keep his words, those who consciously live in the enjoyment of the Father's complacency, and who have fellowship with the Father and with the Son by the Spirit. To these privileged individuals, God reveals himself in his triune personality, and to them he will make known all that is in his covenant of love and mercy.

This expression also implies *a sacred friendship;* for, when God comes to dwell with men, he does not thus dwell with his enemies, but only with those who love him, and between whom and himself there is mutual sympathy. O beloved, if God the Father and God the Son shall indeed come to dwell with us, it will be to us a proof of wondrous love, and dear familiarity, and intense friendship! If you go to live with an earthly friend, it is quite possible for you to stay too long, and to outstay your welcome. But God knows all about the man with whom he comes to live, and Jesus says, "We will make our abode with him," because he knows that his Spirit has purified and sanctified that heart, and made it ready to receive himself, and his Father, too. You remember how Jeremiah pleaded with the Lord not merely to be as a sojourner : "O the hope of Israel, the Saviour thereof in time of trouble, why shouldest thou be as a stranger in the land, and as a wayfaring man that turneth aside to tarry for a night?" But this is not the way that the Father and the Son deal with us, for Jesus says that they will make their abode with us. Does not this imply a very sacred friendship indeed between God and our soul?

It also reveals *the complete acceptance of the man before God ;* for, when anyone comes to stay with you, it is taken for granted that you exercise hospitality towards him ; he eats and drinks in your house ; and, for the time, he makes himself at home with you. "But," you ask, " is it possible that God should accept the hospitality of man?" Yes, it is; listen to the words of Christ himself : "Behold, I stand at the door, and knock : if any man hear my voice, and open the door, I will come in to him, and will sup with him, and he with me." Oh, the blessedness of thus entertaining the King of kings ! Then will he drink of my milk and my wine, and eat the pleasant fruits that are grown in the garden of my soul. Will that which I present to him be acceptable to him? It must be, or else he would not live in my house? And when the Father and the Son come to dwell in the soul of the believer, then all that he does will be accepted ; if he is himself accepted, his thoughts and his words, his prayers and his praises, his almsgiving and his labours for Christ will be accepted by both the Father and the Son.

What a blessed state for anyone to reach ! For then it shall come to pass that this reception, on God's part, from us, shall be followed by a sevenfold reception, on our part, from him. You do not imagine, I hope, that, when God the Father and God the Son make their abode in a man, that the man will continue to be just as he was when they came to him. No, my brethren ; the Lord pays well for his lodging ; where he stays, he turns everything that he touches into gold. When he comes into a human heart, it may be dark, but he floods it with the light of heaven. It may have been cold before, but he warms it with the glow of his almighty love. A man without the indwelling of God is like the bush in Horeb when it was only a bush ; but when the Father and the Son come to him, then it is with him as when the bush burned with fire, yet was not consumed. The Lord brings heaven to you when he comes to you, and you are rich beyond the intents of bliss. All things are yours, for you are Christ's, and Christ is God's, and Christ and God have come to make their abode with you.

Now, according to our Lord's promise, " We will come to him, and will make our abode with him, it is implied that *there they mean to stop.* Let me take your thoughts back, for a minute, to the earlier links in this blessed gospel chain, and remind you that it is only " *if a man love me,*" and it is only " *if he keep my words,*" that the Saviour's promise applies: "We will come unto him, and make our abode with him." Have the Father and the Son come to your heart? Then, I charge you, do nothing that might cause them to depart from you even for a moment. If you ever get into conscious enjoyment of the divine indwelling, be jealous of your heart lest it should ever from your Lord depart, or drive him from you. Say, with the spouse, "I charge you, O daughters of Jerusalem, that ye stir not up, nor awake my love, until he please."

"But," perhaps you ask, "can we keep him? Can we keep him always?" I believe you can. By the blessed help of the Divine Spirit, who has taught you to love him, and to keep his words, you may have near and dear fellowship with your Lord by the month and by the year together. I am sure that we have too low a standard of the possibilities of Christian fellowship, and Christian enjoyment, and Christian living. Aim at the highest conceivable degree of holiness; and, though you will not be perfect, never excuse yourselves because you are not. Always aim at something higher and yet higher still than you have already reached; ask the Lord to come and abide with you for ever. You will be happy Christians if you attain to this privilege, and keep in that condition; and we shall be a blessed church if the most or all of us should attain to it. I mean to go in for this blessing, by God's gracious help; will not you, my brother, my sister? Can any of you be content to live a lower life than is possible to you? I hope you will not be; but that you will reach all of these steps that I have pointed out to you, and ask God in prayer to help you to surmount them. "Lord, help me to love Jesus. Set my soul on fire with love to him. Lord, enable me to keep all his words, and never to trifle with his truth in anything. And then, Father, look upon me with complacency. Make me such that thou canst take delight in me. See the resemblance to thy Son in me, because thou hast made me to be like him; and then, Father, and Saviour, come and abide with me for ever and ever. Amen." Such a prayer as that, truly presented, will be answered, and the Lord shall get glory from it.

But, alas! many of you have nothing to do with this text because you do not love Christ; and the first thing you have to do is not to think about loving him, but about trusting him, for you know that the only way of salvation is by trusting Christ; so, if you do not trust him, you are not in the way of salvation. Have you ever thought of what is involved in being an unbeliever? The apostle John says, "he that believeth not God hath made him a liar; because he believeth not the record that God gave of his Son." Do you really mean to make God out to be a liar? Surely, you cannot; the very thought is too horrible to be entertained for a moment. Well, then, believe his record concerning his Son. That record declares that he is the propitiation for our sins; then, if you rely upon that propitiation, and trust to him who made it, you are saved.

I often have the remark made to me, by an anxious soul, "But, sir, I cannot believe; I wish I could." This is the answer which I generally give to the person who says that:—"What! you cannot believe? Come, now, let us have that matter out. You cannot believe God? Could you believe me?" Of course, the answer is, "Oh, yes, sir; I can believe you!" I reply,—"Yes, I suppose that is because you have confidence in my character, and believe that I would not tell you a lie. Then, in the name of everything that is good and reasonable, how is it that you dare say that you cannot believe God? Is he a liar? Has he ever given you any cause to say to him, 'I cannot believe you'? What do you mean? Give me some reason why you cannot believe God? What has he done that you cannot believe him?" Well, they do not quite see it in that light; but, still, they return to that sentence, "I cannot believe." Well now, sinner, if Jesus Christ were present, and he were to say to you, "Trust me, and I will save you; believe my promise, and you shall enter into eternal life; " would you look him in the face, and say, "I cannot believe thee"? And if he asked you the question, "Why canst thou not believe me?" what would be your reply? Surely, a man can believe what is true. There have been times, with me, since I have known the Saviour, when it seemed to me as if I could not doubt my Lord,—as if I could not find a reason, even if I ransacked heaven, and earth, and hell, why I should doubt him. I protest that I do not know any reason why I should not trust Christ; I cannot conceive of any. Well, will men continue this monstrous, unjust, ungenerous conduct? Alas, they will.

"But," says someone, "if I do trust my soul to Christ, will he save me?" Try him, and see; you have his own promise that he will cast out none who come unto him. So, if thou believest in the Lord Jesus Christ this very moment,—this very moment thou art saved. What more need I say? May the Blessed Spirit cause you to cease, by your unbelief, from practically making God a liar, and may you now come and trust in Jesus, the Substitute and Surety for his people! So shall you rest your weary hearts upon his loving bosom, and it shall be well with you for ever and ever. May God bless you all, for Jesus Christ's sake! Amen.

9. Love at Leisure

" Mary, which also sat at Jesus' feet, and heard his word."—Luke x. 39.

MARY was full of a love to Christ which could be very active and self-sacrificing. I have read to you of her pouring the precious box of spikenard upon our Lord for his anointing. She was therefore one who not only waited and listened, but she served the Lord after her sort and fashion. If she had been simply contemplative and nothing more, we might, perhaps, have considered her somewhat of a one-sided character, and while pointing to that which was good in her as an example, we might have had to comment on her deficiencies, but she did more than sit at the Master's feet. Beloved, if we ever serve the Lord as Mary did, we shall do well.

Now, since she was able thus to serve, she becomes a safe example for us in this other matter of restful faith. The portion of her life occupied in sitting at her Master's feet may instruct and help us. I feel I can safely hold her up to you as an example in all respects, and the more so because, for the particular incident just now before us, she received the Master's express commendation. He praised her also for bringing the box of ointment, but, on this occasion, he praised her too, saying that she had chosen the good part which should not be taken from her. He could not have more conspicuously set his seal of approbation on her conduct than he did. I am not going to say much about her, but I want to speak to those of you who love the Lord as Mary did, to try if I cannot entice you for your own rest and for your own encouragement into following her example in this particular incident, namely, that of sitting at the feet of the Lord Jesus Christ. I have already said you can see that the example is only part of her life—one side of it; at another time I may take the other side, and exhort you to follow her also in that; but for this next hour or so, I want you to leave out the other side of her character and stick only to this. Consider it well, for I am persuaded that this is the true preparation for the other,—that contemplation and rest at the Saviour's feet will give

89

you strength which will enable you afterwards to anoint his feet according as your heart's love shall dictate.

On this occasion, then, we have only to do with Mary sitting at our Saviour's feet. There shall be four heads which you will not forget:—love at leisure sitting down; love in lowliness, sitting at Jesus' feet; love listening—she heard his words; love learning—she heard his words to most blessed purpose: all the while she chose the good part.

I. First, then, LOVE AT LEISURE. That is a point which I want you specially to notice. You that have families to feed and clothe, know how, all day long, you are busy—very busy, perhaps; the husband is away from early morning till the evening comes; the children have gone to school, and the wife is occupied in a hundred household things. But now the evening meal is over, and there is a warm fire burning on the hearth. Is it not one of the most pleasant sights of English interiors to see the family gathered around the fire, just to sit still for a little while to talk, and to indulge in those domestic loves which are the charm of that sweet English word "home"? May an Englishman never cease to think of the word "home" as the most musical word that ever dropped from mortal lips! Now love is quiet and still, and, I was about to say, careless. Outside it has to watch its words, but inside it is playful, it is at ease, it disports itself, fearless of all adversaries. It takes its rest. The armour is put off, and the soldier feels the day's battle is done. He stands not on his guard any longer. He is amongst those that love him, and he feels that he is free. I do not know what life would be if there were not some of those sweet leisure moments when love has nothing else to do except to love—those intervals, those oases in the desert of life, wherein to love is to be happy, and to be loved is to be doubly blest.

Now, Christian people ought to have such times. *Let us put aside our service for awhile.* I am afraid that even those who are busy in the Master's work and are not occupied much with lower things, yet overlook the necessity for love to be at leisure. Now to-night, at any rate, you that work longest and toil most, and have to think the hardest, can ask the Lord to make this a leisure time between you and Jesus. You are not called upon to help Martha to prepare the banquet. Just sit still now—sit still and rest at Jesus' feet, and let nothing else occupy the next hour, but sitting still and loving and being loved by him.

Can we not get rid of worldly cares? We have had enough of them during the six days: let us cast the whole burden of them upon our Lord. Let us roll them up and leave them all at the throne of grace. They will keep till to-morrow, and there is no doubt whatever that they will plague us enough then, unless we have faith enough to master them. But now put them on the shelf. Say, "I have nothing to do with you now—any one of you. You may just be quiet. My soul has gone away from you, up to the Saviour's bosom, there to rest and to delight herself in him."

And then *let us try to banish all church cares also.* Holy cares should not always trouble us. As I came here just now, I said to myself, "I will try to-night not to think about how I shall preach, or how this part of the sermon may suit one class of my hearers or that part another. I will just be like Lazarus was, of whom it is written that 'Lazarus was one of them that sat at the table with him.'" You know that the preacher to such a congregation as this may often find himself like Martha, cumbered with much serving if he forgets that he is but a servant of the Master, and has only to do his bidding. You may well excuse us. But it must not be so to-night. Whether you are deacon or elder, or preacher, or hearer, you must have nothing to do to-night with anything outside of our blessed Lord and our own hearts. Our love shall claim this time for her own rest. No, Martha, even though you are getting ready to feast Christ, we will not hear the clatter of dishes or the preparation of the festival. We must now sit just there at his feet, and look up, and have no eyes except for him, no ears except for him, no heart except for him. It shall be love's leisure night to-night.

And, in truth, beloved, we have plenty of reason for resting. *Let us sit at Jesus' feet because our salvation is complete.* He said, "It is finished," and he knew that he had wrought it all. The ransom-price is paid for thee, O my soul; not one drop has been withheld of the blood that is thy purchase. The robe of righteousness is woven from top to bottom; there is not one thread for thee to add. It is written, "Ye are complete in him," and however frail we be, yet are we "perfect in Christ Jesus," and in spite of all our sin we are "accepted in the beloved." If it be so, O love, hast thou not room for leisure; is not this thought a divan upon which thou mayest stretch thyself, and find that there is space enough for thee to take thy fullest ease? Thy rest is not like the peace of the ungodly of whom it is said, "The bed is shorter than that a man may stretch himself upon it." Here is perfect rest for thee; a couch long enough and broad enough for all thy need. And if, perchance, thou shouldest remember, O my heart, that thou hast sin yet to overcome, and corruption within thee yet to combat, bethink thee this night that Christ has put away all thy sin, for he is "the end of the law for righteousness to everyone that believeth," and that he has overcome the world on thy behalf, and said to thee, "Be of good cheer." Thou hast to fight, but thy foe is a routed foe. It is a broken-headed dragon that thou hast to go to battle with, and the victory is sure, for thy Saviour has pledged himself to it. Thou mayest well take thy leisure, for the past is blotted out and the future is secure. Thou art a member of Christ's body, and as such thou canst not die. Thou art a sheep of his pasture, and as such he will never lose thee. Thou art a jewel of his crown, and as such he will never take his eye or his heart off from thee. Surely then thou mayest take thy leisure.

Let us rest also because we have received so much from our Master. Be sure to remember, O heart that wouldest have leisure for love, that though thou hast many mercies to receive, there are not so many to come as thou hast had already. Thou hast great things yet to learn, but not such great things as thou hast been taught already. He that has found Christ Jesus to be his Saviour has found more than he will ever find again, even though he find a heaven, since even heaven itself is in the loins of Christ, and he that getteth Jesus hath got an eternity of bliss in him. If God gave thee Christ, all else is small compared with the gift thou already hast. Take thy leisure, then, and rejoice in thy Lord himself and in his infinite perfections.

As to the Lord's work, we may well take leisure for love, because it is his work. It will go on rightly enough. It is his work, the saving of those souls. It is well that we are so eager; it were better if we were more eager. But just now we may lay even our eagerness aside, for it is not ours to save: it is his, and he will do it. He will give you soon to see of the travail of his soul. Christ will not die in vain. Election's decree shall not be frustrated, and redemption's purpose shall not be turned aside. Therefore rest.

Besides, my heart, *what canst thou do, after all?* Thou art so little and so altogether insignificant; if thou dost worry thyself into thy grave what canst thou accomplish? God did well enough before thou wert born, and he will do well enough when thou art gone home. Therefore fret not thyself. I have sometimes heard of ministers that have been quite exhausted by the preparation of a single sermon for the Sunday. I am told, indeed, that one sermon on a Sunday is as much as any man can possibly prepare. It is such laborious work to elaborate a sermon. And then I say to myself, "Did my Lord and Master require his servants to preach such sermons as that." Is it not probable that they would do a great deal more good, if they never tried to do any such fine things, but just talked out of their hearts of the simplest truths of his blessed gospel. I turn to the Old Testament, and I find that he told his priests to wear white linen, but he also told them never to wear anything that caused sweat, from which I gather that he did not want his priests in the temple to be puffing and blowing and sweating and toiling like a set of negro slaves. He meant that his service, although they threw their strength into it, should never be wearisome to them. He is not a task-master, like Pharaoh, exacting his tale of bricks, and then again a double tale, giving his servants no straw wherewith to make them. No, but he says, "Take my yoke upon you, and learn of me, for I am meek and lowly in heart and ye shall find rest unto your souls. For my yoke is easy and my burden is light." Therefore it seems to me that, with all the work his people do—and they ought to do it so as to pour their whole life on his head like a box of precious spikenard, yet he did not mean them to go up and down about his service, stewing and worrying and killing their very lives out of them about this and that and the other. They will do his service a great deal better if they will very often come and sit down at his feet, and say, "Now I have nothing to do but to love him—nothing to do but to receive his love into my soul." Oh, if you will seek after such quiet communion you will be sure to work with a holy might that shall consume you. First take in the strength by having these blessed leisures at the Saviour's feet. "He that believeth shall not make haste." He shall have such peace and restfulness, such quiet and calm, that he shall be in no hurry of fear or fright, but he shall be like the great Eternal who, with all that he doeth—and he worketh hitherto, and guideth the whole universe which is full of stupendous wonders—yet never breaks the eternal leisure in which his supreme mind for ever dwells.

Well, if we cannot keep up such leisure as that, at least let us have it to-night. I invite you, persuade you, and entreat you, beloved Marys and others like you, to do nothing but just enjoy the leisure of love, and sit at Jesus' feet.

II. The second thing is LOVE IN ITS LOWLINESS. Love wants to spend her time with Christ: she picks her place, and her place is down at his feet. She doth not come to sit at the table with him, like Lazarus, but she sitteth down on the ground at his feet.

Observe that *love in this case does not take the position of honour*. She is not a busy housewife, managing affairs, but a lowly worshipper who can only love. Some of us have to be managers for Christ; managing this and managing that; but perhaps love is most at home when she forgets that she has anything to manage. She leaves it to manage itself, or better still, she trusts the Lord to manage it all, and just subsides from a manager into a disciple, from a worker into a penitent, from a giver forth into a receiver, from a somebody, which grace has made her, to a nobody, glad to be nothing, content to be at his feet, just to let him be everything, while self sinks and sinks away. Do not let me only talk about this, beloved, but let it be done. Love your Lord now. Let your hearts remember him. Behold his robes of love, all crimsoned with his heart's blood. You shall take your choice whether you look up to him on the cross, or on the throne. Let it be as suits your mind best to-night; but in any case say unto him, "Lord, what am I, and what is my father's house, that thou hast loved me so?"

Sit near thy Lord, but sit at his feet. Let such words as these be upon thy lip, "Lord, I am not worthy to be called by thy grace. I am not worthy to be written in thy book of life. I am not worthy that thou shouldest waste a thought on me, much less that thou shouldest shed thy blood for me. I do remember now what I was when thou didst first deal with me. I was cold, careless and hard towards thee, but very wanton and eager towards the world, giving my heart away to a thousand lovers, and seeking comfort anywhere except in thee. And when thou didst come to me, I did not receive thee. When thou didst knock at my door, I did not open to thee, though thy head was wet with dew and thy locks with the drops of the night. And, oh! since through thy grace I have admitted thee, and thou and I have been joined together in bonds of blessed union, yet how ill have I treated thee! O my Lord! how little have I done for thee! How little have I loved thee! I could faint in thy presence to think that if thou didst examine me and cross-question me, I could not answer thee one of a thousand of the questions thou mightest ask of me. Thy book accuses me of negligence in reading it. Thy throne of grace accuses me of slackness in prayer. The assemblies of thy people accuse me that I have not been hearty in worshipping. There is nothing, either in providence or in nature, or in grace, but what might bring some accusation against me. The world itself might blame me that my example so little rebukes it; and my very family might charge that I do not bless my household as I should." That is right, dear brother, or sister. Sink; go on sinking; be little; be less; be less still; be still less; be least of all; be nothing.

Lift up thine eyes from thy lowly place to him who merits all thy praise. Say to him, "But what art thou, beloved, that thou shouldest have thought of me, or ever the earth was, that thou shouldest take me to thyself to be thine, and then for me shouldest leave the royalties of heaven for the poverties of earth, and shouldest even go down to the grave that thou mightest lift me up and make me to sit with thee at thy right hand? Oh! what wonders thou hast wrought on me; and I am not worthy of the least of thy mercies; and yet thou hast given me great and unspeakable blessings. If thou hadst only let me be a doorkeeper in thy house, I had been happy; but thou hast set me among princes. If thou hadst given me the crumbs from thy table, as dogs are fed, I had been satisfied; but thou hast put me among the children. If thou hadst said that I might just stand outside the gates of heaven now and then, on gala days, to hear thy voice, it would have been bliss for me; but now thou hast promised me that I shall be with thee where thou art, to behold thy glory and to be a partaker of it, world without end." Does not such thoughts as these make you sink? I do not know how it is with you, but, the more I think of the Lord's mercies, the more I grow downward. I could weep to think that he should lavish so much on one that gives him no return at all, for so it seems to my heart that it is with me. What do you think of yourself? What are your faith, your love, your liberality, your prayers, your works? Dare you call them anything? Do you imagine that the Lord is pleased with your past? Would he not rather say to you, "Thou hast bought me no sweet cane with money, neither hast thou filled me with the fat of thy sacrifices; but thou hast made me to serve with thy sins and wearied me with thy iniquities." So we sit down again at his feet, and from that place we would not wish to rise. Love's leisure shall be spent in acts of humiliation. We will bow at the feet that were pierced for our redemption.

III. But now, in the third place, here is LOVE LISTENING. She is down there in the place of humility, but she is where she can catch each word as it falls, and she is there with that object. She wishes to hear all that Christ has to say, and she wishes to hear it close at hand. She wants to hear the very tones in which he speaks and the accents with which he delivers each precept. She loves to look up and see that eye which has such meaning in it, and that blessed countenance which speaks as much as the lips themselves; and so she sits there, and she looks with her eyes toward him as a handmaid's eyes are to her mistress; and then, with her ears and her eyes, she drinks in what he has to say.

Now, beloved, I want you just to do that. Say in prayer now, "Speak, Lord, for thy servant heareth;" and then with your ear open *hear what he says by his word.* Perhaps there is some text that has come home to your soul to-day. Hear it. Hear it well. It would not be much use for anyone to try to preach a sermon in the centre of the city in the middle of the day. If you stood near St. Paul's Cathedral, with all that traffic going by, and all that rumbling, roaring, and shouting, why, the big bell itself might speak, and you would hardly hear it. But when it is night, and all is still, then you can hear the city clocks strike; and you might hear a man's voice even though it was not a very strong one, if he went through the streets, and delivered a message with which he had been entrusted. Well, our blessed Lord often takes advantage of those quiet times when the man has a broken leg, and cannot get to work, but must be still in the hospital, or when the woman is unable to get about the house, to attend to her ordinary duties, but is so helpless that she cannot do anything else but think. Then comes the Lord, and he begins to bring to our remembrance what we have done in days past, and to talk with us as he never has the opportunity of doing at any other time. But it is far more blessed to find time ourselves, so that the Lord will not need to afflict us in order to get us quickly at his feet. Oftentimes the Good Shepherd in caring for the sheep " *maketh* us lie down," but he is glad when we come of our own accord that we may rest and listen to his word.

Listen to what he is saying to you by providence. Perhaps a dear child is sick at home, or you have losses and crosses in business. It may not seem to you as if these things come from your loving Lord, but they are perhaps the pressure of his hand to draw you to his side that he may tell you his secret. Perhaps it has been mercy that has come to you in another way. You have been prospered, you have been converted, you have had much joy in your family. Well, the Lord has a voice in all that he does to his people; so listen to-night. If you listen you will be obliged to say, " What shall I render to the Lord for his benefits to me? "

Listen also to what the Spirit says in your soul. Listen, for it is not till you get your soul quiet that you can hear what the Spirit of God is saying. I have known such a clatter of worldliness or pride, or some other noise, in the soul of man, that the still small voice of the Holy Spirit has been drowned, to the serious detriment of the disciple. Now, I hope you have really done with all your cares and left them outside the Tabernacle to-night, that even the cares about your class in the Sunday-school and about your preaching engagement to-morrow, and everything else, have been put aside, and that now you are just sitting down at Jesus' feet, and listening. While you listen in that fashion, in lowly spirit at his feet, you are likely to hear him say some word to you which, perhaps, may change the whole tenor of your life. I do not know what God the Lord will speak, but " he will speak peace to his people." Sometimes he speaketh in such a way that a turbid life has become clear; a life of perplexity has become decided and distinctly happy; and a life of weakness has become a career of strength; and a life that seemed wasted for a while has suddenly sprung up into eminent usefulness.

Keep thine ear open, Mary. Keep thy ear open, brother, and thou wilt hear what Jesus Christ has to speak.

But now let me say, while you are sitting and listening, *you will do well to listen as much to him as to what he has to say,* for Christ himself is the Word and his whole life is a voice. Oh, sit you down, sit down and listen. I wish I had not to talk to-night, and could sit down and do it for myself, and just look up at him, God over all, blessed for ever, and yet brother to my soul, a partaker of flesh and blood! This very fact, that He is incarnate, speaks to me, that God is in human flesh speaks comfort to my soul, such as no words could ever convey. God in my nature, God become my brother, my helper, my head, my all! Could not my soul leap out of the body for joy at the incarnation, if there were nothing else but that revealed to us?

Now let me look up again, and see my Lord with the wounds, as Mary did not see him, but as we now may, with hands and feet pierced, with scarred side and marred visage, tokens of the ransom-price paid in his pangs and griefs and death. Is it not wonderful to see thy sin for ever blotted out, and blotted out so fully, and blotted out by such means as this! Why, if there were not an audible word, those wounds are mouths which speak his love. The most eloquent mouths that ever spoke are the wounds of Christ. Listen! listen! Every drop of blood says, " Peace "; every wound says, " Pardon ; life, eternal life."

And now see thy beloved once again. He is risen from the dead, and his wounds bleed no more ; yea, he has gone into the glory, and he sits at the right hand of God, even of the Father. It is well for thee, dear brother or sister, that thou canst not literally sit at his feet in that guise, for if thou couldest only see him as he is, I know what would happen unto thee—even that which happened unto John when he saw him with his head and his hair white like wool, as white as snow, and his eyes as a flame of fire, and his feet as if they burned in a furnace. Thou wouldest swoon away. John says, " When I saw him I fell at his feet as dead." You cannot sit at those feet of glory till you have left this mortal clay, or until it has been made like unto his glorious body ; but you may in faith do so, and what will his glory say to you? It will say, " This is what you shall receive ; this is what you shall share ; this is what you shall see for ever and ever." He will say to you—even to you who mourn your insignificance and in lowliness sit at his feet—" Beloved, thou shalt partake of the glory which the Father gave me, even that which I had with him before the world was. Soon, when a few more moons have waxed and waned, soon thou shalt be with me where I am." Oh, what bliss is this! Never mind Martha's frowns ; forget her for the moment and keep on sitting at Jesus' feet. She may come in and grumble, and say that something is neglected ; tell her she should not neglect it then ; but now your business is not with plates or pots, but to do as your Master has permitted you to do, namely, to sit at his feet and listen to him.

IV. So I close by saying, in the fourth place, that here is LOVE LEARNING. Whilst she listened she was being taught, because as she sat at Jesus' feet with her heart all warm—sitting in the posture of lowliness—she was, as few could hear them, *hearing his words so as to spy out their secret meaning.* You know the difference between a man's voice at a distance, saying something, and his being very near you. You know how much the face can say, and the eyes can say, and the lips can say; and there is many a deaf man that has heard another speak though he has never heard a sound; he has known the meaning by the very motion of the lips and the gleams of the countenance. Ah, and if you get into such near fellowship with Christ as to sit at his feet, you will get his meaning. When the letter kills others, you will see the secret meaning that is hidden within, and you will rejoice.

She got at his meaning, and then she was *hearing the words so as to drink in the meaning.* "They sit down at thy feet," says the old Scripture, "every one shall receive of thy words." Beloved, that is a great promise—to receive of his words. Some people hear the words, but do not receive them, but there sat Mary where, as the words fell, they dropped upon her as snowflakes drop into the sea and are absorbed. So each word of Jesus dropped into her soul, and became part and parcel of her nature, they fired and filled her very being.

What she learnt she remembered. We see *love learning what she will treasure up.* Mary never forgot what she heard that day. It remained with her for ever; it seasoned her whole life. The words of her Master were with her all the days she was watching, all the days she was waiting, she was waiting after they had been spoken. They kept her watching and waiting, till at last love's instinct told her that the time was come, and then she went upstairs where she had put away the choice ointment for which she spent her money. She had laid it up and kept it till the time should come, and just before the Saviour's death and burial she fetched it down, the gift which she had hoarded up for him, and she poured it out in adoration.

As she sat at his feet, she resolved to love him more and more. *Love was learning to love better.* As she had listened and learnt, the learning had crystallized itself into resolves to be, among women, the most devoted to him. Perhaps, little by little, she had laid by this great price which she had paid for the spikenard. Be it as it may, it was dear to her, and she brought it down when the time was come, and put it all on him with a joyous liberality and love. Well, now, I want you just to learn of Jesus after that fashion, and, by-and-by, when the time comes, you, too, may do some deed for Christ that shall fill the house in which you dwell with sweet perfume; yea, shall fill the earth with it, so that, if man scents it not, yet God himself shall be delighted with the fragrance you pour, out of love, upon his Son.

We are going to have the communion, here are the emblems of his blessed body and blood; and I hope they will help us to have nothing to do but to think of him; nothing to do but to be lowly in his presence; nothing to do but to listen to his words and to drink in his teaching.

But there are some here that do not love him. It may be that God will lay you low by affliction in order to bring you to the feet of Jesus. Perhaps he will allow disaster and disappointment to overtake you in the world, to win you to himself. If any of you have had this experience, or are passing through it just now, do not trifle with it, I pray you; for, while we are in this life, if the Lord comes to us to remind us of our sin, he does it in the greatness of his mercy, and in order that he may bring salvation to us. It will be quite another thing, in the next life, if you die unrepentant and unforgiven. Then you may indeed dread the coming of God to bring your sin to remembrance; but while you are here, if the Lord is so speaking to you, incline your ear, and hearken to his voice, however harshly it may seem to sound in your ears. Even if he should strip thee, be glad to be stripped by him. If he should wound thee, and bruise thee, willingly give thyself up to be wounded and bruised by him; yea, even if he should slay thee, rejoice to be slain by him, for remember that he clothes those whom he strips, he heals those whom he wounds, and he makes alive those whom he kills. So it is a blessed thing to undergo all those terrible operations of law-work at the hands of the Most High, for it is in that way that he comes to those whom he means to bless.

I cannot preach to you, for the time has gone; but, do you know, I think one of the most dreadful things that can ever be said of man is that he does not love Christ. I should be sorry to enter on my list of friends the man that did not love his mother; yea, I would not call him a man. Dead is that heart to every noble sentiment that loves not her that bare him; and yet there might be some justifiable cause to excuse even that. But not to love the Christ, the God that stooped to bleed for man—this is inexcusable. I dare not to-night utter, as my own, what Paul said, but, very pointedly and solemnly, I would remind you who love not Christ of it. Paul says, " If any man love not the Lord Jesus Christ, let him be anathema Maran-atha "—cursed at the coming. Sometimes when I think of my Lord, and my heart grows hot with admiration of his self-denying love, I think I could almost invoke the imprecation on the head of him that does not, would not, could not love the Christ of God. But better than that I will ask his blessing for you, and I say, " Father, forgive them, for they know not what they do ! "

Here our sermon closes, and may God's blessing rest on it.

10. Christinh the Tree of Life

"In the midst of the street of it, and on either side of the river, was there the tree of life, which bare twelve manner of fruits, and yielded her fruit every month: and the leaves of the tree were for the healing of the nations."—Revelation xxii. 2.*

You will remember that, in the first paradise, there was a tree of life in the midst of the garden. When Adam had offended, and was driven out, God said, "Lest he put forth his hand, and take of the tree of life, and eat, and live for ever, therefore the Lord God drove out the man." It has been supposed, by some, that this tree of life in the garden of Eden was intended to be the means of continuing man in immortality, that his feeding upon it would have supported him in the vigour of unfailing youth, preserved him from exposure to decay, and imparted, by a spiritual regeneration, the seal of perpetuity to his constitution. I do not know about that. If it were so, I can understand the reason why God would not have the first man, Adam, become immortal in the lapsed state he was then in, but ordained that the old nature should die, and that the immortality should be given to a new nature, which should be formed under another leadership, and quickened by another Spirit.

The text tells us that, in the centre of the new paradise, the perfect paradise of God, from which the saints shall never be driven, seeing it is to be our perpetual heritage, there is also a tree of life. But here we translate the metaphor; we do not understand that tree to be literal. We believe our Lord Jesus Christ to be none other than that tree of life, whose leaves are for the healing of the nations. We can scarcely conceive of any other interpretation, as this seems to us to be so full of meaning, and to afford us such unspeakable satisfaction.

At any rate, beloved, if this be not the absolute purpose of the sublime vision that John saw, it is most certainly true that our Lord Jesus Christ is life from the dead, and life to his own living people. He is all in all to them; and by him, and by him alone, must their spiritual life be maintained. We are right enough, then, in saying that Jesus Christ is a tree of life, and we shall so speak of him in the hope that some may come and pluck of the fruit, and eat and live for ever. Our desire shall be so to use the sacred allegory that some poor dying soul may be encouraged to lay hold on eternal life by laying hold on Jesus Christ.

First, *we shall take the tree of life in the winter with no fruit on it ;* secondly, *we shall try to show you the tree of life budding and blossoming ;* and, thirdly, *we shall endeavour to show you the way to partake of its fruits.*

I. And first, my brethren, I have to speak to you of JESUS CHRIST, THE TREE OF LIFE IN THE WINTER.

You will at once anticipate that I mean, by this figure, to describe *Jesus in his sufferings,* in his dark wintry days, when he did hang upon the cross, and bleed, and die; when he had no honour from men, and no respect from any; when even God the Father hid his face from him for a season, and he was made sin for us, that we might be made the righteousness of God in him. My dear friends, you will never see the tree of life aright unless you first look at the cross. It was there that this tree gathered strength to bring forth its after-fruit. It was there, we say, that Jesus Christ, by his glorious merits and his wondrous work achieved upon the cross, obtained power to become the Redeemer of our souls, and the Captain of our salvation.

Come with me, then, by faith, to the foot of the little mound of Calvary, and let us look up and see this thing that came to pass. Let us turn aside as Moses did when the bush burned, and see this great sight. It is the greatest marvel that ever earth, or hell, or heaven beheld, and we may well spend a few minutes in beholding it.

Our Lord Jesus, the ever-living, the immortal, the eternal, became man, and, being found in fashion as a man, he humbled himself, and died the death of the cross. That death was not on his own account. His humanity had no need to die. He might have lived on, and have seen no death if so he had willed. He had committed no offence, no sin, and therefore no punishment could fall upon him.

> "For sins not his own
> He died to atone."

Every pang upon the cross was substitutionary; and for you, ye sons of men, the Prince of glory bled, the Just for the unjust, that he might bring you to God. There was no smart for himself, for his Father loved him with a love ineffable; and he deserved no blows from his Father's hand, but his smarts were for the sins of his enemies, for your sins and mine, that by his stripes we might be healed, and that through his wounds reconciliation might be made with God.

Think, then, of the Saviour's death upon the cross. Mark ye well that *it was an accursed death.* There were many ways by which men might die, but there was only one death which God pronounced to be accursed. He did not say, " Cursed is he that dies by stoning, or by the sword, or by a millstone being fastened about his neck, or by being eaten of worms," but it was written, " Cursed is every one that hangeth on a tree." By no other death than that one, which God did single out as the death of the accursed, could Jesus Christ die. Admire it, believer, that Jesus Christ should be made a curse for us. Admire, and love; let your faith and your gratitude blend together.

It was a death *of the most ignominious kind.* The Roman law subjected only felons to it, and I believe not even felons unless they were slaves. A freed Roman must not so die, nor a subject of any of the kingdoms that Rome had conquered, but only the slave who was bought and sold in the market could be put to this death. The Jews counted Jesus worthy to be sold as a slave, and then they put him to a slave's death for you.

Besides, they added to the natural scorn of the death *their own ridicule.* Some passed by, and wagged their heads. Some stood still, and thrust out their tongues at him. Others sat down, and watched him there, and satisfied their malice and their scorn. He was made the centre of all sorts of ridicule and shame. He was the drunkard's song, and even they that were crucified with him reviled him. And all this he suffered for us. Our sin was shameful, and he was made to be a shame for us. We had disgraced ourselves, and dishonoured God, and therefore Jesus was joined with the wicked in his death, and made as vile as they.

Besides, *the death was exceedingly painful.* We must not forget the pangs of the Saviour's body, for I believe, when we begin to depreciate the corporeal sufferings, we very soon begin to drag down the spiritual sufferings too. It must be a fearful death by which to die, when the tender hands and feet are pierced, and when the bones are dislocated by the jar of erecting the cross, and when the fever sets in, and the mouth becomes hot as an oven, and the tongue is swollen in the mouth, and the only moisture given is vinegar mingled with gall. Ah, beloved! the pangs that Jesus knew, none of us can guess. We believe that Hart has well described it when he says that he bore—

"All that incarnate God could bear,
With strength enough, and none to spare."

You cannot tell the price of griefs, and groans, and sighs, and heartbreakings, and soul-tearings, and rendings of the spirit, which Jesus had to pay that he might redeem us from our iniquities.

It was a lingeriny death. However painful a death may be, it is always satisfactory to think that it is soon over. When a man is hanged, after our English custom, or the head is taken from the body, the pain may be great for the instant, but it is soon over and gone. But in crucifixion a man lives so long that, when Pilate heard that the Saviour was dead, he marvelled that he was dead already. I remember hearing a missionary say that he saw a man in Burmah crucified, and that he was alive two days after having been nailed to the cross; and I believe there are authenticated stories of persons who have been taken down from the cross after having hung for forty-eight hours, and after all have had their wounds healed, and have lived for years. It was a lingering death that the Saviour had to die.

O my brethren, if you put these items together, they make up a ghastly total, which ought to press upon our hearts,—if we are believers, in the form of grateful affection, or if we are unbelievers, provoking us to shame that we do not love him who loved the sons of men so much.

And *the death of the Lord Jesus Christ for us*, we must also add, *was penal.* He died the death of the condemned. Perhaps most men would feel this to be the worst feature; for, if a man shall die by never so painful a death, if it be accidental, it misses the sting which must come into it if it be caused by law, and especially if it be brought by sin, and after sentence has been passed in due form. Now, our Lord Jesus Christ was condemned by the civil and ecclesiastical tribunals of the country to die. And what was more, " it pleased the Lord to bruise him ; he hath put him to grief." Jesus Christ died without any sin of his own, yet he died a penal death, because our sins were counted as his. He took upon him our iniquities as though they were his own, and then, being found in the sinner's place, he suffered, as if he had been a sinner, the wrath that was due for sin.

Beloved, I wish it were in my power to set forth Christ crucified,—Christ visibly crucified amongst you! Oh, that I could so paint him that the eyes of your heart could see him! I wish that I could make you feel the dolour of his griefs, and sip that bitter cup which he had to drain to the dregs. But if I cannot do this, it shall suffice me to say that *that death is the only hope for sinners.* Those wounds of his are the gates to heaven. The smarts and sufferings of Immanuel are the only expiatory sacrifice for human guilt. O ye who would be saved, turn your eyes hither! Look unto him, and be ye saved, all the ends of the earth. There is life in a look at him; but there is life nowhere else. Despise him, and you perish. Accept him, and you shall never perish, neither shall all the powers of hell prevail against you. Come, guilty souls! Jesus wants not your tears or your blood; his tears can cleanse you; his blood can purify you. If your heart be not as broken as you would have it, it is his broken heart, not yours, that shall merit heaven for you. If you cannot be what you would, he was for you what God would have him to be. God is contented with him, so be you also contented with him; and come and trust him. Oh, now may delays be over, and difficulties all be solved, and just as you are, without one plea, but that the Saviour bled, come to your heavenly Father, and you shall be "accepted in the Beloved."

Thus, then, Jesus Christ hanging on the cross is the tree of life in its winter time.

II. And now let me show you, as I may be enabled, THAT SELFSAME TREE OF LIFE WHEN IT HAD BLOSSOMED AND BROUGHT FORTH FRUIT.

There he stands,—Jesus,—still the same Jesus,—and yet how changed! The same Jesus, but clothed with honour instead of shame, able now to save them to the uttermost that come unto God by him. My text says of this tree that it bears "twelve manner of fruits." I suppose that is intended to signify that a perfect and complete assortment of all supplies for human necessities is to be found in Christ,—all sorts of mercies for all sorts of sinners; all kinds of blessings to suit all kinds of necessities. We read, of the palm tree, that every bit of it is useful, from its root to its fruit. So is it with the Lord Jesus Christ. There is nothing in him that we could afford to do without. There is nothing about Jesus that is extraneous or superfluous. You can put him to use in every part, in every office, in every relationship.

A tree of life is for food. Some trees yield rich fruit. Adam in the garden lived only on the fruit of the garden. *Jesus Christ is the food of his people,* and what dainties they have! What satisfying food, what plenteous food, what sweet food, what food precisely suitable to all the wants of their souls Jesus is! As for manna, it was angels' food; but what shall I say of Christ? He is more than that, for—

> "Never did angels taste above,
> Redeeming grace and dying love."

Oh, how richly you are fed! The flesh of God's own Son is the spiritual meat of every heir of heaven. Hungry souls, come to Jesus if you would be fed.

Jesus gives his people drink also. There are some tropical trees which, as soon as they are tapped, yield liquids as sweet and rich as milk, and many drink and are refreshed by them. Jesus Christ's heart blood is the wine of his people. The atonement which he has perfected by his sufferings is the golden cup out of which they drink, and drink again, till their mourning souls are made glad, and their fainting hearts are strengthened and refreshed. Jesus gives us the water of life, the wines on the lees well refined, the wine and milk, without money and without price. What a tree of life to yield us both meat and drink!

Jesus is a tree of life yielding clothing too. Adam went to the fig tree for his garments, and the fig leaves yielded him such covering as they could. But we come to Christ, and we find, not fig leaves, but a robe of righteousness that is matchless for its beauty, comely in its proportions, one which will never wear out, which exactly suits to cover our nakedness from head to foot, and when we put it on makes us fair to look upon, even as Christ himself. O ye who would be rearrayed till ye shall be fit to stand amongst the courtiers of the skies, come ye to Jesus, and find garments such as you need upon this tree of life!

This tree also yields medicine. " The leaves of the tree were for the healing of the nations." Lay a plaster upon any wound, and if it be but the plaster of King Jesus, it will heal it. But one promise from his lips, but one leaf from this tree, but one word from his Spirit, but one drop of his blood, and this is heaven's court-plaster indeed. It is true that there was no balm in Gilead, there was no physician there; and, therefore, the hurt of the daughter of Israel's people was not healed. But there *is* balm in Jesus, there *is* a Physician at Calvary, and the hurt of the daughter of God's people shall be healed if she will but fly to Jesus Christ for healing.

And what shall I more say? Is there anything else your spirits can want? O children of God, Christ is all! O ye ungodly ones, who have been roaming through the wood to find the tree that should supply your wants, stop here. This " apple tree *among the trees of the wood " is the tree which your souls require. Stay here, and you shall have all that you need. For listen,—*this tree yields a shelter from the storm.* Other trees are dangerous when the tempest howls; but he that shelters beneath the tree of the Lord Jesus shall find that all the thunder-bolts of God shall fly by him, and do him no injury. He cannot be hurt who clings to Jesus. Heaven and earth should sooner pass away than a soul be lost that hides beneath the boughs of this tree. And oh, you who have hidden there to shelter from the wrath of God, let me remind you that in every other kind of danger it will also yield you shelter; and if you are not in danger, yet still in the hot days of care you shall find the shade of it to be cool and genial. The spouse in Solomon's Song said, " I sat down under his shadow with great delight, and his fruit was sweet to my taste." Get Christ, and you have got comfort, joy, peace, and liberty; and when the trouble comes, you shall find shelter and deliverance by coming near to him.

He is the tree of life, then, yielding twelve manner of fruits, those fruits being always ripe and always ready, for they ripen every month, all being free to all who desire them, for the leaves are not for the healing of some, but " for the healing of the nations." What a large word! Then there are enough of these leaves for the healing of all the nations that shall ever come into the world. Oh, may God grant that none of you may die from spiritual sickness when these leaves can heal you, and may none of you be filling yourselves with the sour grapes of this world, the poisonous grapes of sin, while the sweet fruits of Christ's love are waiting, which would refresh you and satisfy you.

III. And now I have to show you HOW TO GET AT THE FRUIT OF THIS TREE OF LIFE.

That is the main matter. Little does it boot to tell that there is fruit, unless we can tell how it can be got at. I wish that all here really wanted to know the way, but I am afraid many care very little about it. Dr. Payson had once been out to tea with one of his people, who had been particularly hospitable to him, and when he was going, the doctor said, "Well, now, madam, you have treated me exceedingly well, but how do you treat my Master?" That is a question I should like to put to some of you. How do you treat my Master? Why, you treat him as if he were not Christ, as if you did not want him. But you do need him. May you find him soon, for when you come to die, you will want him then, and perhaps then you may not find him.

Well, *the way to get the fruit from this tree is by faith.* That is the hand that plucks the golden apples. Canst thou believe? That is the thing. Canst thou believe that Jesus is the Son of God, that he died upon the cross? "Yes," sayest thou, "I believe that." Canst thou believe that, in consequence of his sufferings, he is able to save? "Ay," sayest thou. Canst thou believe that he will save thee? Wilt thou trust him to save thee? If so, thou art saved. If thy soul comes to Jesus, and says, "My Lord, I believe in thee, that thou art able to save to the uttermost, and now I throw myself upon thee," that is faith.

When Mr. Andrew Fuller was going to preach before an Association, he rode to the meeting on his horse. There had been a good deal of rain, and the rivers were very much swollen. He got to one river which he had to cross. He looked at it, and he was half afraid of the strong current, as he did not know the depth. A farmer, who happened to be standing by, said, "It is all right, Mr. Fuller; you will get through it all right, sir; the horse will keep its feet." Mr. Fuller went in, and the water got up to the girth, and then up to the saddle, and he began to get uncomfortably wet. Mr. Fuller thought he had better turn round, and he was going to do so when the same farmer shouted, "Go on, Mr. Fuller; go on; I know it is all right;" and Mr. Fuller said, "Then I will go on; I will go by faith." Now, sinner, it is very like that with you. You think that your sins are so deep that Christ will never be able to carry you over them; but I say to you,—It is all right, sinner; trust Jesus, and he will carry you through hell itself, if that is needful. If you had all the sins of all the men that have ever lived, and they were all yours, if you could trust him, Jesus Christ would carry you through the current of all that sin. It is all right, man! Only trust Christ. The river may be deep, but Christ's love is deeper still. It is all right, man! Do not let the devil make you doubt my Lord and Master. He is a liar from the beginning, and the father of lies, but my Master is faithful and true. Rest on him, and all will be well. The waves may roll, the river may seem to be deeper than you thought it to be,—and rest assured it is much deeper than you know it to be;—

but the almighty arm of Jesus—that strong arm that can shake the heavens and the earth, and move the pillars thereof as Samson moved the pillars of Gaza's gates,—that strong arm can hold you up, and bear you safely through, if you do but cling to it, and rest on it. O soul, rest in Jesus, and you are saved!

Once again. *If at the first you do not seem to get the fruit from this tree, shake it by prayer.* "Oh!" say you, "I have been praying." Yes, but a tree does not always drop its fruit at the first shake you give it. Shake it again, man; give it another shake! And sometimes, when the tree is loaded, and is pretty firm in the earth, you have to shake it to and fro, and at last you plant your feet, and get a hold of it, and shake it with might and main, till you strain every muscle and sinew to get the fruit down. And that is the way to pray. Shake the tree of life until the mercy drops into your lap. Christ loves for men to beg hard of him. You cannot be too importunate. That which might be disagreeable to your fellow-creatures when you beg of them, will be agreeable to Christ. Oh, get ye to your chambers, get ye to your chambers, ye that have not found Christ; get to your bed-sides, to your little closets, and "seek the Lord while he may be found, call ye upon him while he is near." May the Spirit of God constrain you to pray. May he constrain you to continue in prayer. Jesus must hear you. The gate of heaven is open to the sturdy knocker that will not take a denial. The Lord enable you so to plead that, at the last, you will be able to say, "Thou hast heard my voice and my supplication; thou hast_inclined thine ear unto me; therefore will I pray unto thee as long as I live."

May God add his blessing to these rambling thoughts, for Jesus' sake! Amen.

11. Our Lord's Preaching

"The LORD hath anointed me to preach good tidings unto the meek; he hath sent me to bind up the brokenhearted."—Isaiah lxi. 1.*

OUR Lord's anointing was with a special view to his preaching. Such honour does the Lord of heaven and earth put upon the ministry of the Word that, as one of the old Puritans said, "God had only one Son, and he made a preacher of him." It should greatly encourage the weakest amongst us, who are preachers of righteousness, to think that the Son of God, the blessed and eternal Word, came into this world that he might preach the same glad tidings which we are called to proclaim.

1.   We may profitably note, first, HOW EARNESTLY OUR LORD KEPT TO HIS WORK.

It was his business to preach, and he did preach, he was always preaching. "What," say you, "did he not work miracles?" Yes, but his miracles were sermons; they were acted discourses, full of instruction. He preached when he was on the mountain, he equally preached when he sat at table in the Pharisee's house. All his actions were significant; he preached by every movement. He preached when he did not speak; his silence was as eloquent as his words. He preached when he gave, and he preached when he received; he was preaching a sermon when he lent his feet to the woman that she might wash them with her tears, and wipe them with the hairs of her head, quite as much as when he was dividing the loaves and the fishes, and feeding the multitude. He preached by his patience before Pilate, for there he witnessed a good confession. He preached from the bloody tree; with hands and feet fastened there, he delivered the most wonderful discourse of justice and of love, of vengeance and of grace, of death and of life, that was ever preached in this poor world. Oh, yes, he preached wondrously, he was always preaching; with all his heart and soul he preached! He prayed that he might obtain strength to preach. He wept in secret that he might the more compassionately speak the word which wipes men's tears away. Always a preacher, he was always ready, in season and out of season, with a good word. As he walked the streets he preached as he went along; and if he sought retirement, and the people thronged him, he sent them not away without a gracious word.

This was his one calling, and this one calling he pursued in the power of the eternal Spirit; and he liked it so well, and thought so much of it, that he trained his eleven friends to the same work, and sent them out to preach as he had done; and then he chose seventy more disciples to go on the same errand. Did he shave the head of one of them to make him a priest? Did he decorate one of them with a gown, or a chasuble, or a biretta? Did he teach one of them to say mass, to swing a censer, or to elevate the host? Did he instruct one of them to regenerate children by baptism? Did he bring them up to chant in surplices and march in processions? No; those things he never thought of, and neither will we. If he had thought of them, it would only have been with utter contempt, for what is there in such childish things? The preaching of the cross—this it is which is to them that perish foolishness, but unto us who are saved it is the wisdom of God, and the power of God; for it pleaseth God still "by the foolishness of preaching to save them that believe." Nor, at the close of his career, had our Lord lowered his estimate of preaching, for, just before he ascended, he said, "Go ye into all the world, and preach the gospel to every creature." His last charge in brief was, "Preach; preach even as I have done before you." He lived the Prince of preachers, he died and became the theme of preachers, he lives again and is the Lord of preachers. What an honourable work is that to which his servants are called!

II.   Secondly, as you have seen that our Saviour came to preach, NOW NOTICE HIS SUBJECT: "The Lord hath anointed me to preach *good tidings* unto the meek."

And what good tidings did he preach? Pardon, pardon given to the chief of sinners, pardon for prodigal sons pressed to their Father's bosom; restoration from their lost estate, as the piece of money was restored to the treasury, and the lost sheep was brought back to the fold. How encouragingly he preached of a life given to men dead in sin, life through the living water which becomes a fountain within the soul! You know how sweetly he would say, "He that believeth on the Son hath everlasting life;"—"He that believeth in me, though he were dead, yet shall he live;"—"As Moses lifted up the serpent in the wilderness, even so must the Son of man be lifted up; that whosoever believeth in him should not perish, but have eternal life." He preached the absolute necessity of a change of heart, and the need of a new creation. He said, "Ye must be born again;" and he taught those truths by which the Holy Ghost works in us, and makes all things new.

He preached glad tidings concerning resurrection, and bade men look for endless bliss by faith in him. He cried, "I am the resurrection and the life; . . . and whosoever liveth and believeth in me shall never die." He gave forth precepts, too, and threatenings in their place,—some of them very searching and terrible; but they were only used as accessories to the good news. He made men feel that they were poor, that they might be willing to be made rich by his grace. He made them feel weary and burdened, that they might come to him for rest; but the sum and substance of what he preached was the gospel,—the good spell,—the glad news.

Brethren, *our divine Lord always preached upon that subject*, and did not stoop to secular themes. If you notice, though he would sometimes debate with Pharisees, Herodians, and others, as needs must be, yet he was soon away from them, and back to his one theme. He baffled them with his wisdom, and then returned to the work he loved, namely, preaching where the publicans and sinners drew near together "for to hear him." Our business, since the Spirit of God is upon us, is not to teach politics, save only in so far as these immediately touch the kingdom of Christ, and there the gospel is the best weapon. Nor is it our business to be preaching mere morals, and rules of duty; our ethics must be drawn from the cross, and begin and end there. We have not so much to declare what men ought to do as to preach the good news of what God has done for them. Nor must we always be preaching certain doctrines, as doctrines, apart from Christ. We are only theologians as far as theology enshrines the gospel. We have one thing to do, and to that one thing we must keep. The old proverb says, "Cobbler, stick to your last;" and, depend upon it, it is good advice to the Christian minister to stick to the gospel, and make no remove from it.

I hope I have always kept to my theme; but I take no credit for it, for I know nothing else; and, like the apostle Paul, I have determined not to know anything among men, save Jesus Christ and him crucified. Indeed, "necessity is laid upon me; yea, woe is unto me, if I preach not the gospel." I would fain have but one eye, and that eye capable of seeing nothing from the pulpit but lost men and the gospel of their salvation; to all else one may well be blind, so that the entire force of the mind may centre on the great essential subject. There is, certainly, enough in the gospel for any one man, enough to fill any one life, to absorb all our thought, emotion, desire, and energy, yea, infinitely more than the most experienced Christian and the most intelligent teacher will ever be able to bring forth. If our Master kept to his one topic, we may wisely do the same; and if any say that we are narrow, let us delight in that blessed narrowness which brings men into the narrow way. If any denounce us as cramped in our ideas, and shut up to one set of truths, let us rejoice to be shut up with Christ, and count it the truest enlargement of our minds. It were well to be bound with cords to his altar, to lose all hearing but for his voice, all seeing but for his light, all life but in his life, all glorying save in his cross. If he who knew all things taught only the one thing needful, his servants may rightly enough do the same. "The Lord hath anointed me," saith he, "to preach good tidings;" in this anointing let us abide.

III.   But NOW NOTICE THE PERSONS TO WHOM HE ESPECIALLY ADDRESSED THE GOOD TIDINGS.

They were "the meek." Just look to the fourth of Luke, and the eighteenth verse, where our Lord was reading this passage in the synagogue at Nazareth, and you will read there, "The Spirit of the Lord is upon me, because he hath anointed me to preach the gospel to the poor." The poor, then, are among the persons intended by the term "the meek." I noticed, when I was looking through various comments upon this passage, that the Syriac renders it "the humble", and I think the Vulgate renders it "the gentle." Calvin translates it "the afflicted." It all comes to one thing. "The meek"—a people who are not lofty in their thoughts, for they have been broken down; a people who are not proud and lifted up, but low in their own esteem; a people who are often much troubled and tossed about in their thoughts; a people who have lost proud hopes and self-conceited joys; a people who seek no high things, crave for no honours, desire no praises, but bow before the Lord in humility; they are fain to creep into any hole to hide themselves, because they have such a sense of insignificance, and worthlessness, and sin. They are a people who are often desponding, and are apt to be driven to despair. The meek, the poor,—meek because they are poor; they would be as bold as others if they had as much as others, or as others think they have; but God has emptied them, and so they have nothing to boast of. They feel the iniquity of their nature, the plague of their hearts; they mourn that in them there dwells no good thing, and oftentimes they think themselves to be the offscouring of all things. They imagine themselves to be more brutish than any man, and quite beneath the Lord's regard; sin weighs them down, and yet they accuse themselves of insensibility and impenitence.

Now, the Lord has anointed the Lord Jesus on purpose to preach the gospel to such as these. If any of you are good and deserving, the gospel is not for you. If any of you fancy that you are keeping God's laws perfectly, and hope to be saved by your works, I have to tell you that the whole have no need of a physician, and that the Lord Jesus did not come upon so needless an errand as that of healing men who have no wounds or diseases. But the sick need a doctor, and Jesus has come in great compassion to remove their sicknesses. The more diseased you are, the more sure you may be that the Saviour came to heal such as you are. The more poor you are, the more certain you may be that Christ came to enrich you; the more sad and sorrowful you are, the more sure you may be that Christ came to comfort you. You nobodies, you who have been turned upside down, and emptied right out, you who are bankrupts and beggars, you who feel yourselves to be clothed with rags, and covered with wounds and bruises and putrefying sores, you who are utterly bad through and through, and know it, and mourn it, and are humbled about it, you may know that God has poured the holy oil without measure upon Christ on purpose that he might deal out mercy to such poor creatures as you are. What a blessing this is! How we ought to rejoice in the anointing of Jesus, since it benefits such despicable objects! We who feel that we are such objects ought to cry, "Hosannah! Blessed is he that cometh in the name of the Lord."

IV. We must now CONSIDER OUR LORD'S DESIGN AND OBJECT IN THUS PREACHING THE GOSPEL TO THE POOR AND THE MEEK.

It was, you observe, that he might bind up the broken-hearted. "He hath sent me to bind up the broken-hearted."

Carefully give heed to the text, so that you may see whether this message applies to you. Are you broken-hearted because of sin; because you have sinned often, foully, grievously? Are you broken-hearted because your heart will not break as you would desire that it should break; broken-hearted because you repent that you cannot repent as you would, and grieved because you cannot grieve enough? Are you broken-hearted because you have not such a sense of sin as you ought to have, and such a deep loathing of it as you perceive that others have? Are you broken-hearted with despair as to self-salvation; broken-hearted because you cannot keep God's law; broken-hearted because you cannot find comfort in ceremonies; broken-hearted because the things which looked best have turned out to be deceptions; broken-hearted because, all the world over, you have found nothing but broken cisterns which can hold no water, which have mocked your thirst when you have gone to them; broken-hearted with longing after peace with God; broken-hearted because prayer does not seem to be answered; broken-hearted because, when you come to hear the gospel, you fear that it is not applied to you with power; broken-hearted because you had a little light, and yet slipped back into darkness; broken-hearted because you are afraid you have committed the unpardonable sin; broken-hearted because of blasphemous thoughts which horrify your mind, and yet will not leave it? I care not why or wherefore you are broken-hearted; Jesus Christ came into the world, sent of God with this object,— "to bind up the broken-hearted."

It is a beautiful figure, this binding up,—as though the Crucified One took the liniment and the strapping, and put it round the broken heart, and with his own dear gentle hand proceeded to close up the wound, and make it cease to bleed. Luke does not tell us that Jesus came to bind up the broken-hearted; if you examine his version of the text, you will read that he came *to heal them*. That is going still further, because you may bind a wound up, and yet fail to cure it, but Jesus never fails in his surgery. He whose own heart was broken knows how to cure broken hearts. I have heard of people dying of a broken heart, but I always bless God when I meet with those who live with a broken heart because it is written, "A broken and a contrite heart, O God, thou will not despise." If you have that broken heart within you, beloved, Christ came to cure you; and he will do it, for he never came in vain: "he shall not fail nor be discouraged." With sovereign power, anointed from on high, he watches for the worst of cases. Heart disease, incurable by man, is his speciality! His gospel touches the root of the soul's ill, the mischief which dwells in that place from whence are the issues of life. With pity, wisdom, power, and condescension he bends over our broken bones; and ere he has done with them, he makes them all to rejoice and sing glory to his holy name. Come then, ye troubled ones, and rely upon your Saviour's healing power. Give yourselves up to his care, confide in his skill, rest in his love. What joy you shall have if you will do this at once! What joy shall I have in knowing that you do so! Above all, what joy will fill the heart of Jesus, the beloved Physician, as he sees you healed by his stripes!

12. Unparalleled Lovingkindnesses

"Lord, where are thy former lovingkindnesses, which thou swarest unto David in thy truth?"—Psalm lxxxix. 49.

THE LORD had made an everlasting covenant with David, ordered in all things and sure, yet that covenant was not intended to preserve him from trouble. When this Psalm was written, he had been brought very low. His crown had been cast down to the ground, his enemies had rejoiced over him, and he had become a reproach to his neighbours. Then his thoughts flew back to the happier days of the past, and the covenant which the Lord had made with him, and either David himself, or Ethan writing on his behalf enquired, in the words of our text, "Lord, where are thy former lovingkindnesses, which thou swarest unto David in thy truth?"

I. Applying this passage to the people of God, I remark, first, that WE HAVE RECEIVED MANY MERCIES IN THE PAST.

Is that too common a matter for you to think and talk about? If you know it so well, why do you forget it so often? The mercies of God wake us every morning, so that we are as used to them as we are to the sunlight, yet some of us think but little of them. They follow us till the night, and we get as accustomed to them as we do to our beds, yet perhaps some of us think less of them than we do of our beds. We have providential mercies every moment of the day, and every day of our lives; we can never tell the number of them, for they are more than the sands upon the seashore. I am going, however, to speak of the spiritual mercies with which God has enriched us,—the blessings of the upper springs; and it will help you to recall them if I take the list of them that is given at the beginning of the 103rd Psalm.

Turn to it, and read, first, *"who forgiveth all thine iniquities."* All of us to whom these words belong should constantly remember that we are pardoned souls. We were not so once; oh, what would we not have given then to know what we do know now? At that time, our iniquities pressed upon us as a burden that we could not bear, the stings of conscience gave us no rest, and the terrors of hell gat hold upon us. When I was under conviction of sin, I felt that I would willingly have given my eyes, my hands, my all, if I might but be able to say, "I am a forgiven soul." So, now that we are pardoned, let us not forget the Lord's lovingkindness in forgiving all our iniquities. If thou, my hearer, canst forget it, I may well question whether thine iniquities have ever been forgiven, for the pardon of sin is so great a mercy that the song which it evokes from the heart must last for ever.

The next mercy in the psalmist's list is, *"who healeth all thy diseases."* Bethink thee again, my brother or my sister, what the Lord hath done for thee in this respect. Once, pride possessed thee, like a burning fever, and long prevented thee from submitting to God's simple plan of salvation; but thou hast been cured of that terrible malady, and now thou art sitting humbly at the feet of Jesus rejoicing in being saved by grace. Perhaps thou wast once like the demoniac of old; the chains of morality could not bind thee, and the fetters of human law could not restrain thee; thou didst cut and wound thyself, and thou wast a terror unto others; but, now, thanks be unto God, thou art so completely healed that there is not even a scar left to show where thou wast wounded. Wilt thou not praise the Lord for this unspeakable mercy? What wouldst thou not have given for it once when thy many diseases held thee in their cruel grip? Then cease not to praise Jehovah-Rophi, "the Lord that healeth thee."

The next mercy also demands a song of grateful praise: *"who redeemeth thy life from destruction."* Thou hast been saved from going down into the pit, the ransom price has been paid for thee, and thou hast been redeemed, not with silver and gold, "but with the precious blood of Christ, as of a lamb without blemish and without spot." Remember that, now, there is no wrath against thee in the heart of God, for his righteous anger on account of thy sin was all poured out upon the head of his dear Son, thy Surety and Substitute. The devil has no claim upon thee now, for thou hast been redeemed by Christ unto the last farthing. Then canst thou forget to praise him who has done such great things for thee? What wouldst thou not have given, at one time, to have had half a hope that thou wert a redeemed soul, when thy poor knees were sore through thy long praying, and thy voice was hoarse with crying unto God? Thou wouldst gladly have bartered the light of day, and the comforts of life, and the joys of friendship for the assurance of thy redemption. Well, then, since thou hast now obtained that priceless boon, forget not to praise the Lord for all his lovingkindness towards thee.

For the next clause in the Psalm is this, *"who crowneth thee with lovingkindness and tender mercies."* Think, brother or sister in Christ, what the Lord hath done for thee. Not content with saving thee from hell, he hath adopted thee into his own family, made thee a son or a daughter of the King of kings, and set a royal crown upon thy head, a crown of "lovingkindness and tender mercies." Thou art made an heir of God, and a joint-heir with Jesus Christ, is not this unparalleled lovingkindness? Is not this indeed the tender mercy of our God towards thee? Then canst thou ever forget such lovingkindness and tender mercy? There have been times, in the past history of some of us, when that ancient prophecy has been most graciously fulfilled in our experience, "Ye shall go out with joy, and be led forth with peace: the mountains and the hills shall break forth before you into singing, and all the trees of the field shall clap their hands." So, as we remember the former lovingkindnesses of the Lord, we rejoice that he still crowneth us with lovingkindness and tender mercies.

We must not forget the next verse: *"who satisfieth thy mouth with good things; so that thy youth is renewed like the eagle's."* If we are in Christ Jesus, we have all that we want, we are perfectly satisfied. We do not want a better Saviour, we do not want a better hope, we do not want a better Bible, we do not want better promises. We do want more faith, but we do not want a better ground of faith. We do desire to have more love to our Lord, but we do not desire a better object for our love. We desire ever to dive deeper and deeper, but only in the fathomless sea of Jesu's love. Others are roaming hither and thither, vainly seeking satisfaction, but our mouth is so filled with good things that we are satisfied. We asked, and the Lord gave unto us. We prayed for pardon, and the Lord fully forgave us for Jesus' sake. We have received so much mercy from him that our soul is satisfied, and soars aloft as on eagle's wings, leaving all terrestrial cares, and sorrows, and doubts far below us amid the earth-born clouds above which we have mounted by God's grace.

II. Now, having thus briefly recalled the Lord's former loving-kindnesses, I have to remind you, in the second place, that WE ARE NOT ALWAYS CONSCIOUS OF THE SAME FLOW OF MERCY TOWARD US.

The psalmist asks, "Lord, where are thy former loving-kindnesses?" Well, where are they? Why, they are where they used to be, though we do not always realize them. The Lord's mercies have not changed, but our perception of them is not always as vivid as it ought to be. Let us again consider the mercies of which I have already spoken to you.

"Who forgiveth all thine iniquities." There are times when a Christian fears whether his sins are really forgiven. He is saved, yet he has a doubt whether he is saved or not. All his past sins seem to rise up before him, and the foul suggestion of unbelief is,

"Can it be possible that all those sins have been put away? Have all those mountains of iniquity been cast into the Red Sea of the Saviour's atoning blood?" Many young believers, who judge themselves too much by their feelings, are apt to imagine that they have been deceived, and that they are still under condemnation. If I have any brethren or sisters like that here, let me assure them that there are times when the very best of the saints have to cry out in the bitterness of their soul, "Lord, where are thy former lovingkindnesses?" The believer in Christ is always justified so far as the law of God is concerned, but he does not always hear the proclamation of pardon in the court of conscience. God's sun is always shining, but there are clouds that obscure its beams, yet it is only hidden for a while. So is it with the lovingkindness of the Lord with regard to the forgiveness of sin; whether we always realize it or not, the forgiveness that has once been bestowed upon us will never be withdrawn from us world without end.

It is the same with the next mercy: "*who healeth all thy diseases.*" It may be that there are some of us here who know that the great Physician has healed our soul maladies, yet at times unbelief and other evil diseases cause us sore pain and agony of spirit. It is with us as it was in the days of Noah when the fountains of the great deep were broken up, and happy are we if we can now float in the ark of our faith above the awful sea of our depravity which threatens to drown every spiritual comfort and cover every hope. If I were to look within my own heart for comfort and hope, I should often be in despair; but when I look away to my Lord alone, then I realize what he has done and is still doing for me, for he still "healeth" all my diseases. Marvel not, dear friends, if you cannot see yourselves growing in grace as you would like to do. When a farmer goes to look at his root-crops, he is not so much concerned as to the appearance of the part that is above ground, he wants to know how that part is flourishing that is out of sight. So, very often, a Christian is growing under ground, as it were,—growing in grace, and knowledge, and love, and humility, though he may not have so many virtues and graces that are visible to other people, or even to himself. Sanctification is being wrought in the saints according to the will of God, but it is a secret work; yet, in due time, the fruit of it will be manifest, even as the farmer at the proper season digs up his roots, and rejoices that his labour has not been expended upon them in vain.

Notice too that next mercy: "*who redeemeth thy life from destruction.*" Now mark this, those who are once redeemed are always redeemed. The price of their redemption was paid upon Calvary, and that great transaction can never be reversed. I dare to put it very strongly, and to say that they were as fully redeemed when they were dead in trespasses and sins as they will be when they stand in the full blaze of Jehovah's presence before the eternal throne. They were not then conscious of their redemption, but their unconsciousness did not alter the fact of their redemption. So is it with the believer; there are dark days and cloudy days in his experience, but he is just as truly saved in the dark and cloudy day as when the sun is shining brightly, and the clouds have all been blown away. In the old days of slavery, when a slave's freedom had been purchased, there may have been times when he had not much to eat, or when he had many aches and pains, but such things did not affect the fact that he was a free man. Suppose someone had said to him, "My poor fellow, you have nothing in the cupboard, you are very sick and ill, you are still a slave;" he would have replied, "That is not good reasoning. I know that I was redeemed, for I saw the price paid for my ransom; I have my free papers, and I shall never again be a slave." So is it with believers, the Son of God hath made them free by giving himself as a ransom for them, so they shall be "free indeed." Their redemption does not depend upon their realization of it, but upon their Redeemer who has made it effective for them.

The same principle applies to the next mercy: "*who crowneth thee with lovingkindness and tender mercies.*" There may be some Christians here who need to learn a lesson that one good Methodist tried to teach another whom he meet at the class-meeting. It grieved him as he heard over and over again the story of his brother's trials and troubles, but nothing about the multitudes of mercies with which he was continually being crowned; so one day he said to him, "My brother, I wish you would change your residence; you do not live in the right part of the town." "How is that?" enquired the other. "Why, you live where I used to live, down in Murmuring Street. It is very dark and narrow, the chimneys always smoke, the lamps never burn brightly there, and all sorts of diseases abound in that unhealthy quarter. I got tired of living in Murmuring Street, so I took a new house in Content Street. It is a fine, wide, open street where the breezes of heaven can freely blow, so the people who dwell there are healthy and happy; and though all the houses in the street are of different sizes, it is a very remarkable thing that they are all of them just the right size for the people who live in them. The apostle Paul used to live in that street, for he said, 'I have learned, in whatsoever state I am, therewith to be content;' so I would advise you, my brother, to move into Content Street as soon as you can." That was very good advice, and we may pass it on to any murmurers or grumblers whom we know. Think, beloved, how the Lord is still crowning you with lovingkindness and tender mercies. I know you are not strong, but then you have not that acute pain you used to have. I know that you are growing old, but that only means that you are getting so much nearer heaven. I know your friends are fewer than they used to be, but then those who are left are true friends. So you see that you are still crowned with lovingkindness and tender mercies.

So is it with the last mercy in the list: "*who satisfieth thy mouth with good things.*" I will venture to say that the Christian has not one real want that is not satisfied with the good things that God has provided for him. If he has any other want, or thinks

he has, it is better for him not to have that want supplied. If
we want the pleasures of sin, it is a great mercy that God will not
give them to us, for the supply of such a want would be our soul's
damnation. If we could gather any comfort through following that
which is evil, it is of the Lord's mercy that such comfort is not
our portion.

> "This world is ours, and worlds to come ;
> Earth is our lodge, and heaven our home ; "

so what can we want beside?

III. Now, thirdly, WHY ARE WE NOT ALWAYS CONSCIOUS OF THE
SAME FLOW OF MERCY TOWARD US?

Sometimes we miss our former comforts as the result of sin.
Sin indulged is a certain barrier to happiness. No one can enjoy
communion with Christ while turning aside to crooked ways. To
the extent to which a believer is inconsistent with his profession,
to that extent will he be unhappy; and it will be no cause for
surprise if he has to cry, "Lord, where are thy former lovingkindnesses?" We must always distinguish between the punishment
of sin which Christ endured on his people's behalf and the fatherly
chastisement with which God's visits upon them their wrong-doing.
Though he will not condemn them as a Judge, he will chastise them
as a Father; and they cannot expect to enjoy the lovingkindnesses
of the Lord while they are enduring the strokes of his rod because
of their transgressions.

We may also lose a comfortable sense of God's mercy *through
neglecting to use the means of grace.* Leave off the regular reading
of your Bible, and then you will be like the man who misses his
meals, and so grows weak and languid. Neglect private prayer,
and then see whether you will not have to cry, with Job, "Oh that
I were as in months past, as in the days when God preserved me;
when his candle shined upon my head, and when by his light I
walked through darkness!" Stop away from the prayer-meeting,
and then, if your soul is not sad, it ought to be. If a man will
not come where there is a fire, is it surprising that he cries that
he cannot get warm? The neglect of the means of grace causes
many to enquire, "Lord, where are thy former lovingkindnesses?"

The same result follows *when any idol is set up in our heart.*
While we worship the Lord alone, the temple of our heart will be
filled with his glory; but if we set up an idol upon his throne, we
shall soon hear the rushing of wings, and the divine voice saying,
"Let us go hence." God and mammon cannot abide in the same
house. Remember that you serve a jealous God, and be very
careful not to provoke him to jealousy. Every idol must be cast
down, or his comfortable presence cannot be enjoyed.

Coldness of heart towards God is another cause of the loss of
enjoyment of his favour. When the heart grows spiritually cold,
the whole being soon gets out of order. If the heart be warm and
vigorous, the pulsations throughout the entire frame will be kept

strong and healthy; but when the heart is cold, the blood will be chilled in the veins, and all the powers will be benumbed and paralyzed. So, beloved, see to it that, in the power of the Holy Spirit, you maintain the love of your espousals, that pristine warmth of holy affection which you delighted to manifest when first you knew the Lord; or else you will soon have to cry, "Lord, where are thy former lovingkindnesses?" Live near to God, and this shall not often be your cry; but if you backslide from him, this shall soon be your sorrowful enquiry. If you have to mourn an absent God, seek to know the reason why he has withdrawn himself from you, and repent of the sin that has separated you from him.

IV. Now, lastly, LET US REMEMBER THAT THE DIVINE COVENANT REMAINS FIRM AND STEADFAST UNDER ALL CHANGING CIRCUMSTANCES. The covenant made with David was established by the oath of God, and Paul, writing to the Hebrews, says that "God, willing more abundantly to shew unto the heirs of promise the immutability of his counsel, confirmed it by an oath; that by two immutable things, in which it was impossible for God to lie, we might have a strong consolation, who have fled for refuge to lay hold upon the hope set before us."

For our consolation, let us remember, first, that the *parties to the covenant are always the same.* God has not one set of chosen ones to-day, and another set to-morrow. In the Lamb's book of life, there are no erasures of certain names, and the insertion of others in their place. No, beloved, that is not the way in which the Lord deals with his elect; he does not play fast and loose with them like that. He does not love them one day, and hate them the next. Oh, no!

> "Whom once he loves, he never leaves,
> But loves them to the end."

And, next, *the seal of the covenant is always the same.* It is sealed with the precious blood of Jesus; his one great sacrifice on Calvary made the covenant for ever sure.

> "'Tis signed, and sealed, and ratified,
> In all things ordered well."

We do not seal the covenant, Christ himself has done that; it is his blood that makes the covenant sure to all for whom he stood as Surety and Substitute. This is our consolation even when we have no present enjoyment of the blessings that are secured to us by the covenant. Even the sealing of the Spirit is not the seal of the covenant, though it is to us the certain evidence of our interest in the covenant; it is like a seal to our copy of the covenant, the great deed itself, sealed with the blood of Jesus, is safely preserved in the archives of heaven where none can mutilate or steal or destroy it.

Further, *the efficacy of the covenant is always the same.* It is not like human covenants, which may or may not be fulfilled, or which may become void through lapse of time. This covenant is eternal, covering past, present, and future, and it shall be fulfilled to the last jot and tittle, for he who sware unto David will certainly perform all that he has promised to his own chosen people.

> "The voice that rolls the stars along
> Speaks all the promises."

When God said, "Let there be light," there was light; and when that same God says, "Let there be light in that dark soul," the light at once enters the heart, and it is divinely illuminated. Thus it has come to pass that we, who were sometimes darkness, now are light in the Lord; and to us comes the apostolic injunction, "Walk as children of light." The efficacy of the covenant does not depend upon us; if it did, it would be a poor, feeble, fickle thing that would fail us just when we needed it most. There would be no hope of our ever getting to heaven if we had to depend upon our own efforts, or our own merits, or anything of our own; our comfort arises from the fact that the covenant is made on our behalf by our great Representative and Redeemer, who will himself see that all that is guaranteed to us in the covenant is fulfilled in due season. There rolls the glorious chariot of salvation, in which all believers are riding to heaven. Death and hell cannot stop it, all the fears of any who are in it will not affect their eternal safety, and not one of them shall be found to be missing in the day when the roll of the redeemed is called in glory. Be of good courage, believer, for thou art saved in the Lord with an everlasting salvation. Even though thou hast for a while to mourn the loss of the Lord's former loving-kindnesses, search thine heart to see how far that loss has been caused by thine own sin, and then return unto the Lord with all thine heart, and he will renew to thee his former favours, and give to thee new mercies of which thou hast not as yet even dreamed.

As for those here who have no former lovingkindnesses of the Lord to which they can look back, I pray that this may be the beginning of better days to them. May they think of the mercies which the Lord has bestowed upon others, and may they cry unto him, "Lord, do to us as thou hast done to them; adopt us also into thy family as thy sons and thy daughters, and let us share in all the blessings that thou givest unto thy children!" Remember, dear friends, that it is by simple and sincere faith in the crucified Christ of Calvary that sinners are eternally saved; it is by his blood that we, who once were afar off, are now made nigh. Whosoever believeth in him shall not be ashamed or confounded; therefore, my hearer, believe thou on the Lord Jesus Christ, and thou shalt be saved, and God shall be glorified. So may it be, for Jesus' sake! Amen.